Games, Ideas and Activities
for Early Years Phonics

Other titles in the series

Games, Ideas and Activities for Early Years Phonics

Gill Coulson and Lynn Cousins

Longman
is an imprint of

Harlow, England • London • New York • Boston • San Francisco • Toronto
Sydney • Tokyo • Singapore • Hong Kong • Seoul • Taipei • New Delhi
Cape Town • Madrid • Mexico City • Amsterdam • Munich • Paris • Milan

Pearson Education Limited
Edinburgh Gate
Harlow CM20 2JE
United Kingdom
Tel: +44 (0)1279 623623
Fax: +44 (0)1279 431059
Website: www.pearsoned.co.uk

First edition published in Great Britain in 2009

© Pearson Education Limited 2009

The right of Gill Coulson and Lynn Cousins to be identified as authors of this work has
been asserted by them in accordance with the Copyright, Designs and Patents Act 1988.

ISBN: 978-1-4082-2435-9

British Library Cataloguing in Publication Data
A CIP catalogue record for this book can be obtained from the British Library

Library of Congress Cataloging in Publication Data
A CIP catalogue record for this book can be obtained from the Library of Congress

10 9 8 7 6 5 4 3 2 1
13 12 11 10 9

Set by 30
Printed and bound in Great Britain by Henry Ling Ltd, Dorchester, Dorset

The Publisher's policy is to use paper manufactured from sustainable forests.

Contents

Introduction

In 2006 the *Independent Review of the Teaching of Early Reading* emphasised the importance of developing speaking and listening skills from birth onwards and recommended systematic, high-quality phonic work as the prime means for teaching beginning readers. As a result, *Letters and Sounds* was published to provide guidance on teaching 'high-quality phonic work' to young children.

Two important features of early phonics teaching are that:

1. Speaking and listening skills are a priority for young children. The more highly developed these skills are, the easier they will find learning to read and write. Opportunities to develop these skills should be a daily focus at the early years stage even when the children have progressed to later stages of the programme.
2. Activities to promote speaking and listening and early phonics teaching should be embedded in all other curriculum area activities. The children should be involved in activities which are play-based and which offer opportunities to talk a lot. This helps them to develop their vocabulary and encourages dialogue with others.

In line with good early years practice, the activities and games in this book are based on play. The activities are lively and fun, many take the children outside as the *Early Years Foundation Stage* recommends. There is a strong emphasis on stories, songs, drama and rhymes, reflecting many of the early learning goals for communication, language and literacy. We also use musical instruments and the environment to encourage children to focus on sounds.

This book provides you with a bank of activities designed to develop your children's speaking and listening skills within a 'broad and rich language experience'. You will find activities suitable for children with different levels of ability. Most of the activities would be ideal for support assistants to use when working with small groups of children who need extra practice, thereby helping classroom teachers and nursery managers with differentiation in their teaching of phonics.

You can follow the ideas in the book to provide daily language-focused games for your children, but it is hoped that the book will soon inspire you to find many more opportunities within your own planning to encourage your children to extend their language skills.

As early years practitioners, you can use this book during your planning, and as you set up and prepare activities for your children. The games and activities are presented under the six aspects of learning from the Early Years Foundation Stage. For each aspect there are two familiar themes containing a range of ideas to promote the development of phonic awareness. You can do the games and activities in any order, as few or as many as you like. Many of the suggestions can be modified to fit your chosen theme. If you don't have copies of the books and poems we have used, simply find another book that has rhyming words or whatever the focus is on – and use that instead.

The games and activities in this book are embedded in all other areas of the curriculum. They are designed to fit in with your existing curriculum, so that you can develop phonic awareness within your planned activities. As such, your phonic awareness teaching will be an integral part of the learning experiences you offer the children, not an add-on, making extra work.

We have built the activities around the things that are happening every day in early years settings. This means that, for example, you don't need to cook in order to teach phonics, but you can use some of these phonic activities because you had already decided to do some cooking. The general idea is that 'while you are doing **that** . . . you can also do **this** phonics activity'.

We have drawn attention to the ways that you can develop language skills, but there are many other potential curriculum learning experiences suggested within the activities and games, and these will enable you to make maximum use of your preparations.

Letters and Sounds

Letters and Sounds is a six-phase teaching programme, compiled by the DfES as part of the National Primary Strategy. It is used with all children from the age of three years, to teach synthetic phonics as a system for learning to read and to spell.

Phase One of *Letters and Sounds* is part (but not all) of the Communication, Language and Literacy (CLL) area of the Early Years Foundation Stage (EYFS). It is designed to help the children tune into sounds, extend their vocabulary and develop their speaking and listening skills

Phase One of *Letters and Sounds* is divided into seven aspects:

Environmental sounds: the sounds that occur around us – from natural sounds like animal noises and weather sounds, to man-made noises such as the sounds of cars and people.
Instrumental sounds: the sounds that we make with home-made or manufactured musical instruments.

Body percussion: using our own bodies to make sounds such as clapping hands, stamping feet or joining in with words and actions in songs.

Rhythm and rhyme: building up a stock of rhymes, poems and songs that the children know, keeping the rhythm correct and being aware of words that rhyme.

Alliteration: exploring groups of words that all start with the same sound.

Voice sounds: using our own voices to create nonsense words and sound effects, and learn about different voices.

Oral blending and segmenting: hearing and saying the phonemes that make up a word, or blending them together to discover the word.

All of the activities in this book were designed around Phase One of *Letters and Sounds*. In addition, some of the activities also cover aspects of Phases Two and Three of *Letters and Sounds*. For example, the activities for oral blending and segmenting will be equally relevant for children working within later phases. Other activities can easily be adapted by including work on letter formation. Many activities provide examples of alternative spelling patterns (graphemes) that could be used as a lively introduction to this later phonic work. All of the activities can be useful for five-minute reinforcement work.

References and resources

We have referred to the terms from *Letters and Sounds – Phase One* throughout the book in the aims and objectives section at the start of each activity. (We changed 'body percussion' to 'sounds we can make' to make it fit the phrasing of our aims and objectives.) If you wish to record this in your planning, then this is the information you will need.

We found it helpful to draw up a list of all the aspects of phonic awareness that the children should experience. This list is based on the aims and assessment opportunities described in Phase One of *Letters and Sounds*, and is included here in case you want to use it in your own planning (see pp. 362–3).

For the most part you won't need specific resources to undertake the activities set out in this book. Where they are needed we highlight this in the resource section at the start of each set of activities.

Teaching phonics

Our language is made up of sounds. There are 44 basic sounds in English, each called a *phoneme*.

Phonemes are shown in the book as /-/, e.g. /a/ or /k/.

As our alphabet has only 26 letters, when we write words we have to use different combinations of these 26 letters to make up the 44 phonemes. These single letters or letter combinations are known as *graphemes*, and are shown throughout as '-', e.g. 'ch' or 'ee'.

Where we have indicated a particular phoneme, we have used the form outlined in *Letters and Sounds*. For more details see *Letters and Sounds, Notes of Guidance for Practitioners and Teachers*, pp.23 and 24.

Remember: When you say any of the phonemes pronounce them as pure sounds, not letter names.

Some sounds (phonemes) may be represented by different combinations of letters (graphemes), e.g, the grapheme (written form) of the phoneme (sound) /k/ can be:

'c' as in cat
'k' as in kitten
'ch' as in chemist
'qu' as in quiche
'ck' as in duck.

The first stage of teaching phonics – called 'phonic awareness' – is about encouraging children to listen purposefully. Children need to recognise that there are lots of different sounds that we make when we speak. They do **not** need to know how to spell them or write them down. That comes later. This matches the guidance given in *Letters and Sounds*.

Early phonics teaching should be a spoken language activity set within play-based learning. Speaking and listening is something that has to be experienced rather than 'taught'. Your aim is to provide a setting where children are immersed in high-quality language experiences, and we hope you find the book helpful in meeting this requirement.

Practitioners and teachers will need to be alert to the opportunities afforded for language development through children's play, and link learning from the *Letters and Sounds* programme with all six areas. (*Letters and Sounds* p. 1)

About the authors

Lynn Cousins was head of an infant school with Beacon status and gained an MA(Ed) in early years education. She has been an editor of educational publications, has written a number of published books, and was involved in compiling *The International Primary Curriculum*.

Gill Coulson was a deputy head of a first school and gained an MPhil degree, researching the teaching of reading. She is currently teaching focused writing groups in a number of local schools.

Authors' acknowledgements

With thanks to the authors of the fantastic stories and poems that have inspired us.

Part 1
Personal, social and emotional development

Chapter 1
Tutti frutti

During their personal, social and emotional development children gain a positive sense of themselves as well as a respect for others. Some of the following phonic activities embrace cultural differences while others encourage children to express preferences and make choices. We have chosen a fruity topic in line with healthy eating policies.

Tip

Before handling or tasting any of the food mentioned please check whether any of the children have allergies.

Handa's Surprise by Eileen Browne

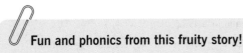

Fun and phonics from this fruity story!

Resources

- A copy of *Handa's Surprise* by Eileen Browne (all activities)
- Pictures of the fruit mentioned in the story – hand drawn or taken from the internet (Activities 2 & 3)
- A shallow basket like the one shown in the story (Activities 2, 3 & 6)
- Examples of real fruit mentioned in the story (Activity 6)

Activity 1

Aims and objectives

- Listening and remembering environmental sounds.
- Learning to imitate sounds.

Preparation

- Read the story *Handa's Surprise* by Eileen Browne.
- Enjoy the story and illustrations.

Tip

Use a big book for sharing with a group of children – it has much more impact!

What to do

- Talk about where the story takes place.
- What differences from our country can they notice, e.g.
  - everyone is wearing cool clothes outside
  - people are carrying baskets on their heads.
- Think about the sounds you would hear if you were there.

- Look at each illustration carefully to see what might be making any sound, e.g.
  - Handa's flip-flops and insects buzzing.
- The animals have to be very quiet when they are stealing the fruit.
- But perhaps you might hear a swipe or a gulp!
- Let the children have fun making some quiet sound effects as you read the story again.

Activity 2

Aims and objectives

- Listening and remembering alliterative sounds.
- Learning to match sounds to objects.

Preparation

- Read the story *Handa's Surprise* by Eileen Browne.
- Enjoy the story and illustrations.
- Have some pictures of the fruit mentioned in the story.
- You will need a basket similar to the one in the story.

Tip

Let the children see the fruit pictures before you start the actual activities.

What to do

- The children sit in a large class circle.
- Look at the pictures of the fruit.
- Remind the children of the names of all the fruit emphasising the initial sound of each name, e.g. – mmm mango.
- Now point to each picture of fruit and say its initial sound – can the children name the fruit?

- Leave the pictures of the fruit on display where the children can see them.
- Place the empty basket on the floor in the centre of the circle.

- Tell the children this is Handa's basket and that you are going to play a remembering game.

- Start by saying, 'In Handa's basket there was a banana.'
- The next child says, 'In Handa's basket there was a banana and a . . .'
- The child can suggest any other fruit from the story, e.g. mango.

- When it is the third child's turn they may need reminding of the fruits already listed.
- Use the initial sound to prompt their memory: /b/ . . . banana, /m/ . . . mango.
- The third child then chooses another fruit to add to the list.
- Carry on playing with each child trying to remember the list and add an item of fruit.

Activity 3

Aims and objectives

- Listening and remembering voice sounds.
- To encourage sustained listening.

Preparation

- Read the story *Handa's Surprise* by Eileen Browne.
- Enjoy the story and illustrations.
- Have some pictures of the fruit mentioned in the story.
- Use a basket similar to the one in the story.

What to do

- Sit in a class circle.
- Put the basket in the centre of the circle with pictures of the fruit inside.
- Remind the children that as Handa walked along she wondered which fruit her friend would like best.

- As you take each picture out of the basket, describe the fruit using the two adjectives used in the story, e.g.
    - the orange was round and juicy.
- When all eight fruits are spread out on the floor, ask a question describing one of the fruits, e.g.
    - who can remember which fruit was round and juicy?
- The child who names the fruit then finds the fruit and puts it back into the basket.
- Continue describing each piece of fruit until all eight pieces are back in the basket.
- Play the game again letting the children take the fruit out when you give its description.
- Continue playing until everyone has had at least one turn.

Tip

Pictures of the fruit are better rather than handling real fruit for these games.

Activity 4

Aims and objectives

- Using language.
- Learning to use adjectives to describe animals.

Preparation

- Read the story *Handa's Surprise* by Eileen Browne.
- Enjoy the story and illustrations.

What to do

- After enjoying the story, remind the children of how the fruit is described in the story: either with two separate words, e.g.
    - tangy, purple passion fruit, or with two hyphenated words, e.g.
    - spiky-leaved pineapple.

- Look again at the illustrations of each animal that steals the fruit. As you show each animal in turn ask the children to think of two words to describe the animal, e.g.
  - long-necked giraffe, or
  - tall, yellow giraffe.
- When each animal has been described show the illustrations again.
- Who can describe the animal AND the fruit they stole!

Tip

The children will find it easier if they play Activity 3 before trying to describe the animals in Activity 4.

Activity 5

Aims and objectives

- Tuning into instrumental sounds.
- Learning to develop awareness of sounds made by different instruments.

Preparation

- Read and enjoy *Handa's Surprise* by Eileen Browne.
- Collect together some percussion instruments, e.g.
  - shakers
  - drums
  - rainmakers
  - tambourines.

What to do

- You are going to tell the story in musical sounds – a little like *Peter and the Wolf*.
- Start by trying to create a sound and rhythm for each animal.
- Choose children to be the eight animals in the story.

- Ask the children to use an instrument to make a sound as their animals steal the fruit. (No animal noises! Remind them that the animals are quiet!)
- Help them to make suitable choices, e.g.
    - a gentle shake of the tambourine as the giraffe makes her way through the tall grass.
- Now choose a child to be Handa who fills the basket with pictures of the fruit.
- They will need to choose a sound to play:
    - as each piece of fruit is put into the basket
    - as she walks to visit her friend.
- Finally choose a sound for the tangerines falling from the tree and filling the basket, e.g.
    - quick soft beats on a drum.
- As you show the pictures, the children can play the sound story.

Activity 6

Aims and objectives

- Tuning into sounds.
- Learning to develop their listening skills.

Preparation

- Read the story *Handa's Surprise* by Eileen Browne.
- Enjoy the story and illustrations.
- Arrange pieces of fruit in a shallow basket.

Tip

Testing and tasting some of the exotic fruits from the story would be an exciting experience for the children and an opportunity to develop their vocabulary as well as their taste buds!

What to do

- This is a listening game where everyone has to be extremely quiet!
- Everyone sits in a big circle around the basket of fruit.
- Choose a child to be Handa who sits in the middle of the circle beside the basket.
- Ask this child to wear a blindfold or simply cover their eyes.

- Another child then has to try and creep up to the basket and lift out a piece of fruit, but if Handa hears them they have to sit down and let someone else try.
- If they manage to lift the fruit from the basket then it's their turn to be Handa.

Fruit salad

Use these activities to encourage children to eat more fruit!

Resources

- A selection of fruit, table, cash register, purses, coins and paper bags (Activity 3)

Tip

All these activities can be adapted to use with a vegetable theme too!

Activity 1

Aims and objectives

- Remembering environmental sounds.
- Learning to imitate and identify environmental sounds.

Tip

Visit a shop with the children to buy fruit for making your fruit salad.

Preparation

- Make a simple fruit salad with the children by cleaning, preparing and cutting up fruit.

What to do

- Sit in a large class circle.
- Talk about the fruits you have sampled and everyone's favourites.
- Tell the children you are going to mime preparing some fruit for the fruit salad.
- Can they guess what you are doing?

Use actions and simple sound effects as you pretend to prepare some fruit, e.g.
  – cutting an orange in half then squeezing the juice from it
  – scooping out the seeds from a passion fruit
  – peeling a banana and slicing it.

- When a child guesses correctly they can have a turn at pretending to prepare some fruit.
- Encourage them to use a few simple sound effects with their actions.

Tip

Try mixing some chopped fruits into plain yoghurt to make your own fruit yoghurts.

Activity 2

Aims and objectives

- Listening and remembering voice sounds.
- Learning to listen for a target word and respond with an action.

What to do

- Sit the children in a large circle and tell them everyone is going to be a fruit.
- Go round the circle giving each child a fruit name repeating three fruits in order, e.g.
  - banana, apple, plum/banana, apple, plum/banana . . .
- Give them time to practise remembering what fruit they are, e.g.
  - say 'All the plums stand up.'
- Now explain to the children how to play the game.
- When you call out one fruit, all those children swap places, e.g. all the plums will change places so that all the plums are in a different place round the circle.

- The fun really starts when you call out **fruit salad!**
- Then everyone stands up and changes places.

Activity 3

Aims and objectives

- Using language.
- Learning to use shopping language.

Preparation

- Set up a shop in your play area.

- You will need:
  - a selection of fruit – real or artificial
  - a table
  - paper bags
  - a cash register
  - some purses with coins in.

What to do

- Talk to the children about places to buy fruit, e.g. market stall/supermarket/greengrocer's.
- Show the children the fruit shop in the classroom.

Working with a small group, choose a child to be the shopkeeper.

- The adult then models the language needed to buy fruit:
  - 'Please can I have three oranges?'
  - 'How much are the grapefruit?'
  - 'I will have two, please'
  - 'That's all for today, thank you.'
- Now give the purses to three children and let them go shopping.
- Take turns being the shopkeeper.

Tip

Shopping is a good opportunity to encourage the use of please and thank you!

Guess the fruit

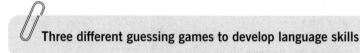

Three different guessing games to develop language skills

Resources

- Four fruits with different initial sounds (Activity 1)
- Number cards, children's own pictures of fruit (Activity 2 variation)

Activity 1

Aims and objectives

- Tuning into alliteration.
- Learning to identify initial sounds in words and reproduce them clearly.

Preparation

- Collect a small selection of familiar fruits (each with a different initial sound).

What to do

- Help the children name the different fruits, e.g.
  - banana, apple, pear, strawberry.
- Ask who can hear what sound apple begins with?
- The child who answers correctly can come to the front and hold the fruit.

- Repeat with the other fruits until you have a child holding each fruit.
- Now ask the children to hold the fruit behind their backs.
- Then they take it in turns to say, 'My fruit begins with . . .' Can the other children guess the fruit?
- Repeat the game until everyone has had a turn.
- Play the game again another day with some different fruits.

Variation

- When the children are familiar with several fruit names and their initial sounds, they can play a simple guessing game without real fruit.
- The teacher can start by introducing the sentence . . .

    'My favourite fruit begins with . . . Can you guess it?'

- The child who guesses the name of the fruit correctly can then repeat the sentence with a different initial sound.

Activity 2

Aims and objectives

- Tuning into rhythm and rhyme.
- Learning to understand the pattern of syllables.

Preparation

- Children need to know the names of a range of fruit before playing this game.

What to do

- Talk about different types of fruit.
- Who has tried what and which do they like most?

- Clap the rhythm of a fruit: say the name and clap the beat.
- Do this with lots of different fruits encouraging the children to join in.

- Sort the fruit into sets according to the number of beats in their name:
    - **1 beat**: plum, pear, peach, grape, lime
    - **2 beats**: apple, orange, mango, cherry, lemon, kiwi, lychee, raisin
    - **3 beats**: banana, pineapple, strawberry, raspberry, blueberry, sultana, apricot
    - **4 beats**: pomegranate, avocado.
- Ask them to guess the fruit from your claps; say yes if a child suggests a fruit with the correct number of beats!
- Then let them have a turn clapping a mystery fruit.

Variation

- Help the children make pictures of a range of fruit.
- Set out four cards numbered – 1, 2, 3, 4.
- Let each child take a card in turn and clap out the rhythm of its name.
- They then place the picture in a pile with the card showing its number of beats or claps.

Tip

For a quick version, play clap and guess at snack time. Can the children guess the fruit for today?

Activity 3

Aims and objectives

- Using language.
- Learning to use descriptive words.

Preparation

- The children need to be familiar with a range of fruits.

What to do

- Tell the children, 'I ate a delicious fruit today. Can you guess what it was?'
- Describe a fruit, e.g.
  - It was small and round, shiny and red.
- Can the children guess which fruit?

Tip

A good game for those odd spare minutes!

- Take the opportunity of introducing more new vocabulary into your descriptions, e.g.
  - tangy, creamy, crinkly-skinned, mottled.

- Once the children understand the idea of the game, let them take turns describing fruits.
- Praise the children if they use adventurous word choices.

Fabulous fruit games

 Develop listening skills as you play indoors or out!

Resources

- Large picture of a pear, plum and apple (Activity 3)

Activity 1

Aims and objectives

- Tuning into sounds.
- Learning to articulate words carefully.

Preparation

- The children need to be familiar with a range of fruits before they can play this game.

What to do

- Sit in a class circle.
- Explain to the children that you are going to pass a whisper around the circle.
- Tell them it's important to whisper but also to say the word very clearly.
- Whisper the name of a fruit to the child on your left.
- Then they have to whisper the same fruit to the next child.
- And so on all the way round the circle.
- When the whisper reaches the child on your right, they whisper it to you. Is it still the same fruit?

Tip

Start by whispering a single word, e.g. pineapple.
If it gets back to you as the same fruit then you can try a short phrase, e.g. soft, purple plum.

Variation

- Choose a child to start off the whisper.

Activity 2

Aims and objectives

- Tuning into alliteration.
- Learning to identify initial sounds in words.

What to do

- Tell the children that the farmer – Old MacDonald – has been growing fruit on his farm.
- Explain that unlike animals, fruits don't make sounds.
- So if he grows pears we are going to say the sound that starts the word pear. We'll sing:

*'With a /p/ /p/ here and a /p/ /p/ there
Here a /p/ there a /p/
Everywhere a /p/ /p/'*

- Stand in a large class circle.
- Choose one child to stand inside the circle – this is the farmer.
- Ask the farmer to choose what fruit he wants to grow.
- Check that the children all know the initial sound of the chosen fruit.
- Then sing the song as you walk around the farmer.

*Old MacDonald had a farm, ee-eye, ee-eye oh
And on that farm he grew some pears, ee-eye, ee-eye oh
With a /p//p/ here and a /p/ /p/ there
Here a /p/ there a /p/
Everywhere a /p/ /p/
Old MacDonald had a farm, ee-eye, ee-eye oh*

- Ask a second farmer to choose what fruit to grow.
- Check that the children all know the initial sound of this fruit.
- Repeat the song, with the initial sound of the second fruit.

- The song can be repeated as long as the children are enjoying it!

Activity 3

Aims and objectives

- Listening and remembering sounds.
- Learning to listen for a target word and respond with an action.

Preparation

- Put a big picture of each of the following fruits in three corners of a large space:

  pear/plum/apple.

Tip

This is a good game to play outside.

What to do

- Use the tune to 'Oats and beans and barley grow'.
- Teach the children the song:

  Pears and plums and apples grow
  Pears and plums and apples grow
  But not you nor I or anyone know
  How pears and plums and apples grow.

- The children skip around while singing the song.
- The adult then calls out 'plums' or 'pears' or 'apples'.
- The children run to the corner where the picture is and jump up and down as if picking the fruit.

- Return to the centre to sing the song again and repeat with a different fruit.
- If the adult calls out, 'dinner's ready', the children run to the fourth area (home) and sit down and pretend to eat their dinner.

Chapter 2
Same or different?

As part of their personal, social and emotional development children will be encouraged to recognise that we all share many similarities but that we also are unique individuals. As you concentrate on these tricky concepts with the children there will be a number of opportunities for you to reinforce their phonic awareness.

Dressing·up

Have fun with your finery as well as your phonics.

Resources

- Dressing-up clothes, including accessories and jewellery (all activities)
- Carrier bags or baskets (Activity 2)

Activity 1

Aims and objectives

- Tuning into alliteration.
- Learning to identify the initial sounds in words.

Preparation

- Sort dressing-up items into pairs according to their initial sound.

What to do

- Explain to the children that in this game they can only wear things that start with the same sound as their name.
- Show the children two items from your dressing-up collection, ask, 'Who can wear these?' Children could respond with lots of suggestions of names.
- You may need to practise saying the names of the objects first, very clearly so that the children can hear the initial sounds. Don't forget – concentrate on the sound, not the spelling!
- Repeat with another two objects until everyone has something to wear.
- Try:
  - hat, handbag – Harry, Henry, Hannah
  - T-shirt, tiara – Tom, Toby, Tracey
  - shawl, shoes – Charlotte, Shani, Sean

- purse, pyjamas – Pete, Patti, Poppy
- crown, cap – Connie, Katy, Connor
- baseball cap, belt – Ben, Becky, Billie
- jacket, jewellery – Jane, Jamie, Jenny.

- If you can't match the dressing-up items to your own children's names let them choose new names that do match the items you are holding up.

Tip

Be inventive in the names you give the objects: 'necklace' might also be 'beads' or 'jewels'; you might use the term 'bag' or 'shopping bag' or 'carrier bag' or 'plastic bag'. This will open up opportunities for more children to be involved.

Activity 2

Aims and objectives

- Tuning into alliteration.
- Learning to identify the initial sounds in words.

Preparation

- Place a number of dressing-up items in bags or baskets. Each one will contain three items that start with the same sound, and two or three other items.

What to do

- Tell the children: 'Harry will only wear things that start with the same sound as his name. What sound is that?' Allow time for the children to work this out.
- Then say, 'In this bag I have some things that Harry will like to wear. Can you find them?'
- Pass the bag to the children who sort through and identify the items and choose the ones that Harry will wear.
- Repeat with other names and other bags of dressing-up clothes.

- Try:
  - Harry: hat, helmet, cap, handbag, scarf
  - Connie: coat, crown, jacket, purse, cap
  - Shelley: scarf, shoes, shorts, waistcoat, shawl
  - Tom: tiara, ring, T-shirt, trousers, wellies.

Activity 3

Aims and objectives

- Listening and remembering alliteration.
- Learning to hear the difference in sounds at the beginning of words.

Preparation

- Into each bag or basket place five items, two of one initial sound, and two of another, plus one rogue item.

What to do

- Choose two children and give them a bag of dressing-up items. They have to choose the ones that are the same initial sound as their own name, and put them on. You may need to explain that there is one thing in the bag that won't match either of their names.
- Try:
  - Tom and Sarah: tiara, trousers, scarf, sandals, necklace
  - Charlotte and Ben: shawl, shirt, belt, bandana, gloves
  - Harry and James: helmet, hat, jewellery, jacket, mittens.

Tip

Improvise names to fit the available dressing-up items if the children's own names won't work.

Name games

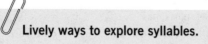

Lively ways to explore syllables.

Resources

- Everyday objects that have 1, 2, 3 or 4 syllables in their names (Activity 2)

Activity 1

Aims and objectives

- Tuning into rhythm and rhyme.
- To understand the pattern of syllables.

What to do

- Clap the rhythm of your name: say the name and clap the beat.
- Do this with lots of the children's names encouraging them to join in.
- Sort children into groups according to the number of beats in their name:
  - **1 beat**: Paul, Ann, Tom
  - **2 beats**: Sarah, Vikash, Danny
  - **3 beats**: Jennifer, Christopher, Jameela
  - **4 beats**: Elizabeth, Sarah-Louise.

Variation

- Once the children know the number of claps in their own name, play this as a game.
- The adult claps 1, 2, 3 or 4 times. If any child has that number of beats/syllables in their name they can stand up. The first child to stand then claps and says his own name.

Activity 2

Aims and objectives

- Tuning into rhythm and rhyme.
- Learning to understand the pattern of syllables.

What to do

- Can the children find some objects in the room that have the same number of beats /claps/ syllables as their name?
- Choose a child, clap the rhythm of his name and count the beats.
- Help the children to identify some objects around the setting that have that number of beats:
  - Sam: door, paint, cube, door, chair, shoe, sink
  - Emma: window, table, model, easel, cupboard, pencil
  - Emily: triangle, wellington, window-sill
  - Elizabeth: painting table, colouring book.

- The adult shows an object, or points to it.
- Ask the children to stand up if they think their name has the same number of beats/syllables as this.
- Say, count and check each time.

- Choose two children with a different number of beats in their names. Identify these with the group. Show two objects. Can the children work out for themselves whose name they match? e.g.
  - The ball matches Sam
  - The pencil matches Barry.

Portraits

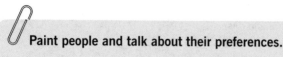

Paint people and talk about their preferences.

Resources

- Paint and paper

Activity 1

Aims and objectives

- Listening and remembering alliteration.
- Learning to suggest objects that start with the same sound.

Preparation

- Invent some characters that the children can paint. These will be used to make a display.

What to do

- Spend time with the children collecting together descriptions. These should use lots of words with the same initial sound.
- Try:
  - Brian is a baker. He likes bread and butter. He has brown eyes and black hair. He likes to ride his bicycle.
  - Charlie makes chocolates. He likes cheese sandwiches. He is always cheery.
  - Prudence is pretty. She likes to wear pink clothes. She has plaits in her hair. She likes to eat pancakes.
- Now paint your characters.

Tip

These may need to be collaborative pictures so that you can help the children. Some of the things the characters like could be made separately and added to the 'person' when the paint is dry.

Activity 2

Aims and objectives

- Listening and remembering alliterative sounds.
- Learning to hear the difference in sounds at the start of words.

Preparation

- Sit together so that the children can see the display of characters you have created for Activity 1 of this section.

What to do

- Remind the children of the characters that you created, and how their names, descriptions and likes and dislikes all start with the same initial sound.
- Thinking about the characters you have created, play an odd-one-out game.
- Try:
  - Does Charlie like chips or beans?
  - Does Prudence sit in a pram or a buggy?
  - Does Bob make bread or cakes?
- Talk about other things that the characters would wear, eat or do, e.g.
  - What else does Charlie like to eat?
    chocolate
    cheese
    chips
    chutney
    chipolatas
    cherries.

  - What else does Bob like to do?
    build
    box
    bathe
    basket ball
    boating
    brush his hair.

  - What else does Prudence like to wear?
    pyjamas
    pants
    pullovers
    party clothes
    pink clothes
    purple clothes
    pretty clothes
    poncho.

Activity 3

Aims and objectives

- Listening and remembering alliteration.
- Learning to suggest objects that start with the same sound.

Preparation

- Children will each paint an alien or monster using only one colour of paint each.

What to do

- Once the paintings are dry you are going to give them each a name, a description and identify some things that they like to eat or do, etc. e.g.
    - A green alien:
        can be: Gordon, Graham, Gavin, Gollum, Grace
        can be : gorgeous, great, good, glad
        and can like: grapes, guns, grasshoppers, geese.
    - A red monster:
        can be: Robbie, Ravi, Rachel, Rosie
        can be: wriggly, rich, rubbery, round
        and can like: rabbits, ravioli, running, racing.

Ring games

Taking turns and sharing as you think about words.

Resources

- PE bands in four colours: blue, red, green, yellow (Activity 2)
- A soft toy that can be passed around (Activity 3)

Activity 1

Aims and objectives

- Tuning into sounds we can make.
- Learning to join in with words and actions in songs.

What to do

- Children dance round in a ring. One child sits in the middle, head in hands.

  Poor Mary sits a-weeping, a-weeping, a-weeping

  Poor Mary sits a-weeping

  On a bright sunny day

- Children stand and wag a finger at Mary as they sing.

  Stand up, and choose a new friend, a new friend, etc.

- Then the child in the centre stands and points to a child who in some way is like themselves, e.g.
  - Both have the same colour of hair
  - Both are wearing jeans
  - Both have shoes with laces
  - Both are girls
  - Both have a pet dog
  - Both like apples.

- The chosen child is 'the friend'.
- Two children in the centre hold both hands crossed and dance round, as the children in the circle clap.
  And now she's got a new friend, a new friend, etc.
- The chosen child now becomes 'Mary'.

Tip

The adult will need to help the child explain their choice of friend.

Activity 2

Aims and objectives

- Tuning into sounds we can make.
- Learning to join in with words and actions in songs.

Preparation

- The flowers in the song are blue, red, green and yellow.
- Give each child a colour using PE colour bands or sticky labels.

What to do

- Use the tune to 'In and out the dusty bluebells'.
- Children form a ring with arms raised.
- Choose two or three children wearing **blue** to weave in and out of the circle of children as they all sing the first verse.

  In and out the bonny bluebells

  In and out the bonny bluebells

  In and out the bonny bluebells

  Who will be my partner?

- The children each stand behind someone else wearing **red** and tap on their shoulders as the children all sing

Pitter patter, pitter patter on your shoulder
Pitter patter, pitter patter on your shoulder
Pitter patter, pitter patter on your shoulder
You will be my partner.

- They swap places and the children in **red** weave in and out as they all sing. Continue in this way choosing a different colour each time and singing the appropriate verse until all of the children have had a turn.

In and out the rambling roses . . .
In and out the graceful grasses . . .
In and out the dainty daffodils . . .

Variation

- One child wearing **blue** dances round to the first verse. He then chooses a child wearing **red**, to hold on to him and they both weave in and out for the second verse. The second child chooses a third child in the colour of the third verse. And so on until the line gets too long for the size of the circle.

Activity 3

Aims and objectives

- Listening and remembering sounds.
- Learning to listen for a target word and respond.

Preparation

- Children should be sitting in a circle.
- Have a soft toy that they can pass round.

What to do

- Pass a soft toy round the circle and count as you pass it on. '1, 2, 3' and the next person, on receiving the soft toy, has to choose another child who in some way is different from them, e.g.
  - trousers/dress
  - blue jumper/red jumper
  - boy/girl
  - long hair/short hair
- These two children swap places in the circle.
- The child holding the toy continues to hold it as they exchange places and then starts passing it on again.

Tip

Encourage the children to tell everyone why they have chosen that person. How are they different?

Is it the same?

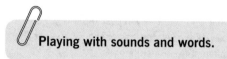

Playing with sounds and words.

Resources

- Chime bars and beaters (Activity 1)

Activity 1

Aims and objectives

- Listening and remembering sounds.
- Learning to identify the differences between sounds.

Preparation

- Collect together a number of chime bars and beaters. Include two of each note.

What to do

- Play a couple of beats on the two chime bars. Ask the children if they are the same.
- If not, which one is higher – the first one or the second one that I play? Play them again to help them decide.
- Vary the chime bars when you repeat it. Sometimes they will be the same note. Sometimes they will be different.
- The children can play this with their friend, taking it in turns to play and guess.

Activity 2

Aims and objectives

- Listening and remembering sounds
- Learning to make up a series of rhyming words.

Preparation

- Sit in a circle.

What to do

- Explain to the children that words that have the same ending rhyme – like boy and toy.
- Tell the children that they are each going to say a word that rhymes with the one the adult says. They can be real words or made up words.
- You start with a word which has lots of simple rhyming words, e.g.
  - **Cat**: bat, rat, hat, sat, mat, fat, pat, gnat
  - **Win**: din, sin, pin, thin, bin, Lynn, skin, chin, fin, tin
  - **Toe**: low, know, row, go, sew, flow, blow, whoa, snow
  - **Bill**: sill, till, will, frill, brill, Gill, nil, fill, kill, pill.
- Allow children to repeat an earlier word if they find it hard to think up a new suggestion.
- Change to a new starter word when ideas are running out.

Activity 3

Aims and objectives

- Tuning into sounds.
- Learning to recognise that some words rhyme and that some words start with the same sound.

What to do

- The adult says three words. The children have to identify the odd one out and explain why.
- The words you say will either:
  - Rhyme/not rhyme, or
  - Start with the same sound/not start with same sound, e.g.
    Adult says: run, star, sky
    Children's response: 'run' is odd because the other two start with /s/.

> Adult says: win, cup, tin
> Children's response: 'cup' is odd because the other two rhyme.
>
> - Other examples could be:
>   dog, frog, wood (wood)
>   jam, jelly, custard (custard)
>   ham, tomato, honey (tomato)
> - You could make it trickier by saying three words with two optional responses, e.g.
>   cat, kitten, rat
>   'kitten' is the odd one out because the other two rhyme
>   'rat' is the odd one out because the other two start with the same sound, /k/.
> - Other examples could be:
>   star, car, caravan
>   pear, share, party
>   Ben, Bob, Ken
>   girl, boat, goat
>   bend, ball, send
>   straw, sticks, bricks.

Pants by Giles Andreae and Nick Sharratt

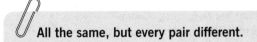

All the same, but every pair different.

Resources

- A copy of *Pants* by Giles Andreae and Nick Sharratt
- Card and wrapping paper to make a huge pair of pants (Activity 3)
- Over-sized pants – all sorts of different shapes and styles – drawn on paper for the children to decorate (Activity 3)

Activity 1

Aims and objectives

- Tuning into rhythm and rhyme.
- Learning to experience and enjoy rhythm and rhyme.

Preparation

- Read the book and share the fun of it.

What to do

- Re-read the book, missing out the occasional rhyming word. Can the children supply you with it?
- Pick out some of the rhymes. You say one of the phrases. Can the children remember its rhyming partner? e.g.
  - 'Groovy pants, funky pants' and 'Cheeky little m . . . pants'
  - tight/night
  - daisy/lazy/crazy
  - funny/money/sunny/bunny

  and all the rest.

Activity 2

Aims and objectives

- Talking about oral blending and segmenting of words.
- Talking about the different phonemes that make up a word.

Preparation

- Read the book with the children. Encourage them to join in.

What to do

- Choose a few of the words and segment them into their basic sounds, e.g.
  - 'fairy' breaks down into /f/ - /air/ - /ee/
- Say these slowly and distinctly, encouraging the children to join in. Count the number of sounds (phonemes). Remember to ignore the spelling at this stage.
- Tell the children that they can do the same with the word 'hairy'. Let them try /h/ - /air/ - /ee/
- Can they also segment 'Mary', 'dairy', 'wary'?

Tip

If the children suggest 'scary' which is a rhyming word in the book, explain that this one has four sounds, not just three. It has /s/ and /k/ sounds before the /air/ sound. It segments as /s/ - /k/ - /air/ - /ee/.

The children may find it quite hard to hear these two separate sounds at the beginning of the word.

Variations

- Other words to try include:

  night: /n/- /igh/ - /t/
  tight: /t/ - /igh/ - /t/

  more: /m/ - /or/
  door: /d/ - /or/

happy: /h/- /a/ - /p/- /ee/
nappy: /n/ - /a/ - /p/ - /ee/

car: /k/ - /ar/
are: /ar/

funny: /f/ - /u/ - /n/ - /ee/
money: /m/ - /u/ - /n/ - /ee/

Activity 3

Aims and objectives

- Talking about sounds.
- Learning to make up a series of rhyming words.

Preparation

- Cut out a pair of large pants from card. Decorate them, colour them or cover the card in a fun wrapping paper.

What to do

- The children are going to think up a long list of rhyming words to describe your pants. 'My pants are . . . pants.' Be as silly as you want. Make up words if you need some extras. This is meant to be fun! e.g.

  'My pants are funny, sunny, runny honey pants.'
  'My pants are silly, frilly chilly pants.'
  'My pants are happy, chappy nappy pants.'

- Children could decorate some wild and whacky pants of their own.

Part 2
Communication, language and literacy

Chapter 3
Pirates

Playing at pirates can inspire boys as well as girls to take part in language-based activities. This theme provides an exciting opportunity to develop children's communication, language and literacy knowledge.

Tip

Do each of these activities dressed as a pirate. If you have square scarves to tie on heads, or long scarves to tie round waists you will be able to turn the children quickly into pirates.

Let's play pirates

An adventurous way to discover phonics.

Resources

- Pirate clothes (All activities)
- Sugar paper (Activities 3 & 4)
- Hoops (Activities 5 & 6)
- Treasure chest (Activity 6)
- Paper flags in different colours (Activity 6)

Activity 1

Aims and objectives

- Tuning into alliteration.
- Learning to make up alliterative phrases.

Preparation

- Help the children to dress up as pirates.

What to do

- Each child is to choose a pirate name – it has to begin with /p/.
- Work together to make a collection of names that start with the same sound as 'pirate', e.g.
    Pete
    Percy
    Polly
    Penny
    Pinky
    Paul

> Prince
> Princess
> Pearl
> Pat
> Patti.
>
> - The children can now choose one of these names for themselves and so become 'Pirate Pete' or 'Pirate Penny'.

Tip

Write the pirate names on sticky labels or you'll forget who's who!

Activity 2

Aims and objectives

- Tuning into sounds we can make.
- Learning to articulate words carefully.

Preparation

- Dress one or two children as pirates and let them sit at the front of a small group of children – in the 'hot seat'.

What to do

- The other children can ask them questions about being a pirate.
  Where do you live?
  Do you like going to sea?
  Do you ever get scared?
  Where did you find the treasure?
  Where did you find the map?
  Was it in the first place you looked?
  What was the treasure?
  What was in the chest?
  Did the captain share it out?

Tip

Have some questions ready to start the ball rolling.

Activity 3

Aims and objectives

- Listening and remembering alliteration.
- Suggesting objects that start with the same sound.

Preparation

- Make your pirate ship from an upturned table or large play bricks, or a huge cardboard box.
- Cut out interesting shapes from coloured paper or fabric to make 'islands'.
- Lay these out.

What to do

- The game starts with everyone on the ship.
- If the pirates can think of something beginning with the same sound as one of the island colours, they can get off the ship and onto that island, e.g.
  - **blue**: bag, brick, ball, balloon
  - **green**: granny, garden, gold, goat
  - **red**: ribbon, reindeer, rain, robin
  - **yellow**: yacht, yolk, yam, yard.

Activity 4

Aims and objectives

- Talking about rhythm and rhyme.
- Learning to make up a series of rhyming words.

Preparation

- Make your pirate ship from an upturned table or large play bricks, or a huge cardboard box.

- Cut out interesting shapes from coloured paper or fabric to make 'islands'.
- Lay these out.

What to do

- All the pirates should be in the 'ship'.
- Ask them for words (real or invented) that rhyme with the colour word of one of the islands. If they can think of one, they get off the ship and sit on that island, e.g.
  - **blue:** moo, Sue, grew, few
  - **green:** seen, bean, lean, mean
  - **red:** bed, head, said, ted
  - **yellow:** fellow, hello, bellow.

Activity 5

Aims and objectives

- Tuning into environmental sounds.
- Learning to develop listening skills.

Preparation

- Spread out differently coloured hoops (several of each colour). These will be 'islands'.

What to do

- Children run around, or 'swim' in the sea and listen . . . the adult calls out one of the colours.
- The children have to get 'onto' that island – but there is only room for three on each island. Anyone not on an island of the right colour has to go back to the 'boat' – identify a place for this at the start of the game.
- Remove one hoop each time until all are on the boat.

Variation

- Children move around freely, 'swimming' in the sea or jumping from 'island' to 'island'.
- When they jump onto an 'island' they have to say their pirate name.

    'I am Pirate Pete and this is my island!'

Tip

This is a good game for outdoors where you can spread out more easily.

Activity 6

Aims and objectives

- Listening and remembering alliteration.
- Learning to recall a list of objects that start with the same sound.

Preparation

- On the day your snack is to be one of these fruits, play this game just before snack-time.
- Prepare a paper flag in the colour that matches the initial sound of your chosen snack, e.g.
    blue – bananas
    red – raisins
    orange – oranges
    green – grapes
    silver – satsumas, sultanas
    pink or purple – peaches, pears.
- One child should be dressed as a pirate and given the paper flag and a treasure chest.
- The chest will contain the day's snack suitably boxed or wrapped. Don't let the children see what this is.

What to do

- Ask the children, 'What colour is the flag?'
- Then ask, 'What sound does that start with?
- Once everyone knows what this is the game can continue.

- Tell the children that whatever is hidden in the treasure chest will begin with this sound.
- The pirate now asks the other children, 'What do you think could be in the chest?'
- The others have to name something that starts with the same sound as the colour of the flag.
- If they get it right they join the pirate.
- When everyone is together the pirate opens the chest to reveal the treasure – the fruit or snack for that session!
- Enjoy your treasure.

Hunt the treasure

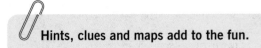

Hints, clues and maps add to the fun.

Resources

- Ribbons (Activity 1)
- Maps (Activity 3)
- Sand tray (Activity 4)
- Small objects (Activity 4)

Tip

Make your own treasure maps. Use diluted tea or coffee (grains or powder) sprinkled on wet paper to make your maps look old.

Activity 1

Aims and objectives

- Tuning into rhythm and rhyme.
- Learning to recognise that some words rhyme.

Preparation

- Set up a treasure hunt in the grounds.
- Decide on a set of clues, rhyming with your hiding places, e.g.
    Look behind something that rhymes with 'flea' (tree)
    Look near something that rhymes with 'wrench' (bench)
    Look under something that rhymes with 'bone' (stone)
    Look on top of something that rhymes with 'chin' (bin)
    Look in something that rhymes with 'band' (sand).
- You will need to hide one item of treasure per child per group in each hiding place.

Tip

Ribbons in bright colours could be your treasure.

What to do

- Divide the children up – three children to one adult would be easy to manage.
- Give each adult a set of two or three simple clues.
- Give each group different clues if you are all playing it at once. The same clues can be repeated if you are working with only one group of children at a time.
- Tell the children one clue at a time.
- The children follow the clues and retrieve the 'treasure'.

Activity 2

Aims and objectives

- Tuning into rhythm and rhyme.
- Learning to recognise that some words rhyme.

Preparation

- Set up a treasure hunt in the grounds.
- Decide on a set of clues, rhyming with your hiding places. (See Activity 1 for ideas.)
- Write the clues out, one per card.
- Keep one clue back as your starter. Place the rest around the grounds. The final clue will lead the children to the 'treasure', so remember to hide that as well.

Tip

Laminate the cards if you want to keep the game for future use.

What to do

- Tell the children the first clue.
- When they get there they will find the card with the second clue on it. The adult reads it to them.

- They follow the clue and this will lead them to the third clue and so on . . . until eventually they find the actual treasure chest.
- Open it up to find a small treat for each child.

- Lay the clues out in different orders when you play again with another group of children.

Activity 3

Aims and objectives

- Using language.
- Learning to ask and answer questions.

Preparation

- Make a large map showing three islands – one small, one medium and one large.
- On each 'island' draw some features, such as: a tree, a house, stones or pebbles.
- Lay it out flat or pin it to your board.
- Make A4 copies of the map – one per child.
- Roll these up like a pirate's treasure map. You could even tie a ribbon round each one.

What to do

- Give a rolled-up map to each of your pirates. Let them decide where the treasure is to be buried and mark it on their map. Keep this out of sight of the other pirates!
- Each pirate now comes to the front in turn and answers questions. Other children have to guess where the treasure is hidden by asking questions – but the pirate who hid it can only answer 'yes' or 'no', e.g.
  Is it in the sea?
  Is it on the big island?
  Is it near the tall tree?
- Repeat the game with the other pirates.

Activity 4

Aims and objectives

- Listening and remembering alliteration.
- Learning to hear the difference in sounds at the beginning of words.

Preparation

- Collect up sets of items that begin with the same sound.
- You will use two sets for each treasure hunt.
- Bury the treasure in the sand tray.

What to do

- Two children at a time will hunt for treasure in the sand.
- Each child will be looking for a different sound at the same time, e.g.
  - bury some things that begin with '/k/ – crayon, cat, comb, king, and some things that begin with /p/ – pot, pencil, plane.
- Tell each child which letter sound to hunt for – and off they go.

Tip

If you want to concentrate on rhyming words, the activity could be adapted using objects from the list in Appendix 2, see pp. 358–9.

What's in the treasure chest?

 All the excitement of opening up a secret.

Resources

All activities need:
- Treasure chest: let the children make a beautifully decorated box as a separate activity
- Small objects, see pages 356–9.
- Hoops or fabric squares to mark sets (Activities 3 & 4)
- 2 sacks or PE bags (Activity 10)
- Music to dance to (Activity 12)

Tip

Each of these activities depends on the careful choosing of objects before the session starts. See pages 356–9 for ideas.

Activity 1

Aims and objectives

- Listening and remembering alliteration.
- Learning to hear the difference in sounds at the beginning of words.

Preparation

- Have five or six objects in the chest. All but one should start with the same initial sound.

What to do

- Take out each object in turn and get the children to identify each one.
- When all are on view ask the children for the one that starts with a different sound, e.g.

ball, biscuit, banana, book, cup
dog, drum, doll, dinosaur, frog
mouse, monkey, mug, spoon
ship, shoe, shell, car.

Activity 2

Aims and objectives

- Listening and remembering alliteration.
- Learning to match sounds to objects.

Preparation

- Put three objects per initial sound in the chest.

What to do

- Take out one object.
- Ask a child to reach in and find another object that starts with the same initial sound as the one you are holding.
- Ask a child to reach in and find an object that starts with a different initial sound from the one you are holding.

Variation

- Each child chooses two objects – UNSEEN – from the chest.
- If they both have the same initial sound, they place them in the middle of the circle of children.
- If they don't match they go back in the chest.
- Continue until all the objects in the chest are paired off.

Activity 3

Aims and objectives

- Tuning into alliteration.
- Learning to identify the initial sounds in words.

Preparation

- Have two sets of objects in the chest, three or four for each initial sound.

What to do

- Have two 'sets' in the middle of the circle of children; these could be formed by hoops, pieces of paper or squares of fabric.
- Place one object in each set to start with. Children should identify the object and its initial sound.
- Each child in turn dips into the chest and removes one object. He names it and then places it in the appropriate set, e.g.
  potato, plum, pencil/cup, car, crayon
  top, tortoise, train/leaf, lid, ladder.

Variation

- Mark the two sets by using differently coloured fabric, hoops or paper.
- Name the colour and say its initial sound.
- Each child finds something in the chest that starts with, e.g. /r/ for red, or /p/ for purple and places the object in the correct set.

Activity 4

Aims and objectives

- Listening and remembering alliteration.
- To suggest objects that start with the same sounds.

Preparation

- Fill the chest with lots of objects, an even number of each initial sound.

What to do

- Each child chooses three objects from the chest – anything they like. Or you may prefer to distribute them to make sure that each child has three different initial sounds.
- Child One chooses one of his objects and places it in the treasure chest. He names it and identifies its initial sound.

- Pass the chest around. Does anyone else have something beginning with this sound? If they do, they place it in the chest, naming it as they do so,
- You now tip all of these objects out into a set in the middle of the circle of children.
- Repeat the game with Child Two choosing one of his objects and everyone else adding a matching item.
- Continue with different children leading until all of the objects are sorted.
- Look at each set in turn and ask the children to name the objects and identify 'What is the same about their names?' *The sound that they start with*. What is that sound?

Activity 5

Aims and objectives

- Listening and remembering alliteration.
- Learning to suggest objects that start with the same sound.

Preparation

- Set out the treasure chest in a prominent place. It should be empty.

What to do

- Start this at the beginning of a morning or afternoon session.
- Tell the children, 'In our treasure chest today we are collecting things that begin with the sound . . .'
- Ask the children to look for objects and place them in the chest over the course of the session.
- At the end of the session you sit round, open the chest and find out what is in it.
- Children can help to identify the objects and assess whether they are right or wrong.
- Can they stay in the treasure chest or not?

Activity 6

Aims and objectives

- Talking about alliteration.
- Learning to select a range of words that start with the same sound.

Preparation

- Put some objects in the treasure chest.

What to do

- Take one object out of the treasure chest and ask the children to name it.
- Get the children to work together to find a word to describe the object that starts with the same sound as the name of the object, e.g.
  red ribbon
  blue brick
  shiny shoe
  big box
  dangerous dinosaur
  beautiful butterfly
  silver spoon.

Tip

Any number of objects could be in the box, but think carefully about what you put in and make the description obvious.

Activity 7

Aims and objectives

- Talking about rhythm and rhyme.
- Learning how to make up a series of rhyming words.

Preparation

- Put the objects you have chosen in the chest.

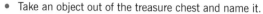

What to do

- Take an object out of the treasure chest and name it.
- Encourage the children to come up with lots of words that rhyme with it. These could be real or made up words, e.g.

  cat: hat, fat, mat, sat, gnat, pat, rat, lat, jat

  dog: log, frog, tog, Mog, sog, rog

  mouse: house, louse, fouse, wouse

  car: star, far, bar, lar, dar

  pear: chair, stare, stair, éclair, mare, fair, hair, hare, wear, tear.

- After you have done this as a group, replace all of the objects into the chest and allow each child in turn to take and name one object and give at least one rhyming word.

Activity 8

Aims and objectives

- Tuning into oral blending and segmenting.
- Learning how to blend phonemes into words.

Preparation

- Place three or four objects in the treasure chest.
- Choose the objects carefully. The children at this stage can find it tricky to hear when two separate consonant sounds follow each other, as in

  's-c' in scarf

  'b-r' in brick

  'd-r' and 'n-k' in drink.

What to do

- Ask the children: 'Can you find the . . .' and segment the word of your chosen object, e.g.

  c-ar

  d-o-g

  l-ea-f

  m-ou-se

sh-oe
s-o-ck
h-a-t
c-u-p
d-o-ll
d-i-sh
c-ow
l-a-mb.

- To do this successfully the child needs to hear/identify the sounds, be able to blend them to make a word and then match the word to an object in the chest.

Tip

Younger children may find it helpful to know what is in the chest before they try this.

Activity 9

Aims and objectives

- Tuning into alliteration.
- Learning to identify the initial sounds in words.

Preparation

- Decide on your chosen letter sound, and have more objects starting with that sound than you will have children in the group, so that everyone will have a choice when it is their turn. Add a few objects starting with any other sound.

Tip

You might want to prepare several sets of objects so that you can play again with another sound. See Appendix 1 (p. 356–7) for ideas.

What to do

- You say the line 'I spy with my little eye something beginning with . . .'
- As you do so, pass the chest round the group. Each child in turn looks in and finds an object that he thinks begins with the sound, before passing the chest on.
- You may have to repeat the 'I spy . . .' words and say the letter sound clearly for all the children to identify and remember the sound that they are looking for.
- When all have chosen, remind them of the sound you were looking for.
- Now go round the group and ask each child to name his object.
- Decide together whether he is right or wrong.
- If he is wrong he can go back to the chest and try again.

Activity 10

Aims and objectives

- Listening and remembering alliteration.
- Learning to hear the difference in sounds at the beginning of words.

Preparation

- Use two sacks or bags.
- Choose pairs of objects that start with the same initial sound and place one of each pair in each bag.

Tip

Try using PE bags in different colours for the sacks.

What to do

- Tell the children that these are the pirates' sacks brought back with them from a treasure hunt. What have they found?
- Two children come out. One child takes an object from one of the bags, and the other takes an object from the second bag.

- Compare them. Do they start with the same initial sound?
    Yes: Put them in the treasure chest
    No: Put them back in the bags.
- Another two children have a turn.
- Keep going until all the pairs are found.

Tip

Put rhyming pairs of objects in the bags, and then play the game when rhyming is your focus.

Activity 11

Aims and objectives

- Listening and remembering alliteration.
- Learning to match sounds to objects.

Preparation

- Choose objects that start with the same sound as places and resources around your room, e.g.
    teddy: table, train set, toilets
    sock: sand-tray, sellotape, scissor block
    wellington: water-tray, window, whiteboard
    shoe: shelf, shop.

What to do

- Each child takes an object of his choice from the box.
- Now tell them that they should go around the room and find something or somewhere that starts with the same sound and leave their object there.
- Come back to the circle when you have done this – but remember where you left it!

- When all are back play a game: 'George had a teddy. Where do you think it is?'
- Children can make suggestions and George can tell them 'right' or 'wrong'.
- When it is guessed correctly George and the one who guessed can go and retrieve the object.

Tip

It's probably best to do this as a whole group activity or you could discover that you have lots of other 'helpful' children who will keep bringing back the objects you have 'lost' around the room!

Activity 12

Aims and objectives

- Tuning into rhythm and rhyme.
- Learning to recognise that some words rhyme.

Preparation

- In the treasure chest place two or four objects for each rhyme. Have enough objects for one per child.

What to do

- Everyone reaches into the chest and takes an object – no looking as you choose!
- Play the music and let the children dance around the room.
- When the music stops you have to find someone who has an object that rhymes with your object.
- Check that all are correct before replacing the objects in the chest and then choosing again.

Tip

You could play it with initial sounds instead of rhyming words.

Activity 13

Aims and objectives

- Listening and remembering alliteration.
- Learning to suggest objects that start with the same sound.

Preparation

- Match the objects you put in the chest to the names of the children who will form the group to play this game, plus a few extras with other starting sounds.

What to do

- Each child in turn says his name and works out the sound it starts with.
- He then looks in the chest to find an object that starts with the same sound.
- When everyone has chosen, and is holding their object, either:
- Each child in turn says what he is called and the name of his object:
     'I am Charlie and I have found chocolate.'
     'I am Ashok and I have found an apple.'
  or:
- The adult asks, 'Who has a car?'
  Children reply: 'Kris has a car.'
  'Who has a frog?'
  'Phoebe has a frog.'

Tip

If the adult leading the game chooses an object from the chest for her own name, she can demonstrate the spoken part of this activity.

Stories, songs and rhymes

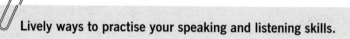

Lively ways to practise your speaking and listening skills.

Resources

- A copy of *Come Away from the Water, Shirley*, by John Burningham (Activity 1).
- Poetry books such as *Blue Poetry Paintbox* or *Singing in the Sun* (Activity 4).

Activity 1

Aims and objectives

- Talking about voice sounds.
- Widening the range of vocabulary needed to talk about the different voice and speech sounds they can make or hear.

Preparation

- Read *Come Away from the Water, Shirley* by John Burningham, making sure the children can see the pictures on facing pages which tell a different story from the story you are reading aloud.

What to do

- Let the children tell the story of Shirley's pirate adventure using the pictures from the book as prompts.
- Think up words for the different characters to say.
- How would they speak?
- Experiment with different voices, and talk about the different voices.
    - Parents?
    - Women?
    - Girls?
    - Men?
    - Old people?
    - Pirates?
- What are their voices like? Describe them and try them out.
- Act out the adventure.

Activity 2

Aims and objectives

- Talking about rhythm and rhyme.
- Learning to create their own rhymes.

What to do

- Sing this traditional song with the children.
  When I was one I banged a drum (mime this)
  Going out to sea (use hand to show rolling waves)
  I climbed aboard a pirate ship (jump)
  And the captain said to me (salute)
  'We're going this way, that way (move left, then right)
  Forward and backward (move forward and backward)
  Over the Irish Sea (show waves)
  A bottle of rum (drink from bottle)
  To fill my tum (rub tummy)
  That's the life for me!'

- Make up new rhymes for the opening lines of each verse:
  When I was one I banged a drum
  I sucked my thumb
  I ate a plum
  When I was two I lost my shoe
  I shouted 'Boo!'
  When I was three I hurt my knee
  I climbed a tree
  I lost the key
  When I was four I knocked at the door
  I sat on the floor
  When I was five I learnt to dive
  I had to drive

Activity 3

Aims and objectives

- Tuning into sounds we can make.
- Learning to join in with words and actions in songs.

What to do

- Learn, sing and act out the traditional song, 'The big ship sails on the alley, alley-O'.
- There are several verses and suitable actions given in *This Little Puffin*. Other publications will offer their own versions.
- Make up some additional verses of your own.
  'The pirates sail to a country far away . . .
  In search of buried treasure'

  'The pirates sail in a very stormy sea . . .'
  'The pirates land on a rocky, rocky shore . . .'
  'The pirates dig in the muddy, muddy ground . . .'
  'The pirates pull out a heavy, heavy chest . . .'

  'The pirates open the rusty, rusty lid . . .
  And they all shout out HURRAH!!!'

Activity 4

Aims and objectives

- Tuning into rhythm and rhyme.
- Learning to understand the pattern of syllables

What to do

- The children may be familiar with the rhyme
  'A sailor went to sea, sea, sea
  To see what he could see, see, see
  But all that he could see, see, see
  Was the bottom of the deep blue sea, sea, sea.'

- Children stand facing a partner and clap their opposing hands in rhythm with the words, working out their own pattern of movements.
- Change 'sailor' to 'pirate' in line one, and the words in the last line. The children need to keep the number of syllables right in order to keep the rhythm, e.g.
  'Were the fishes in the deep, blue sea, sea, sea'
  'Were the waves on the deep blue sea . . .'
  'Was a mermaid in the deep blue sea . . .'

Activity 5

Aims and objectives

- Tuning into rhythm and rhyme.
- To experience and enjoy rhythm and rhyme.

What to do

- There are lots of poems about pirates. Read them to the children, encouraging the children to join in as you read them again.
- Ask the children to supply the rhyming words as you read the poems out.
- Children may be able to memorise some short poems if you read them again and again over several days.
- Some suggestions:
  - *Blue Poetry Paintbox*:
    'There was an old pirate' by Wendy Larmont
    'I wish I was a pirate' by Tony Bradman.
  - *Singing in the sun*:
    'Sailing to sea' by Dennis Lee.

Chapter 4
Nursery rhymes

Many early years practitioners already teach nursery rhymes to their children because they are an excellent way to introduce communication, language and literacy. In the following activities we have used five traditional favourites as a basis for developing rhythm and rhyme.

'Hickory dickory dock'

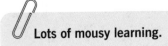

Lots of mousy learning.

Resources

- Collection of different-sized clocks or pictures (Activity 1)
- Picture or model of a grandfather clock and a finger puppet mouse (Activity 3)
- Toy pig and toy mouse (Activity 8)

Activity 1

Aims and objectives

- Listening and remembering environmental sounds.
- Learning to imitate sounds.

Preparation

- Have a collection of different-sized clocks for the children to investigate and notice the different sizes. Use pictures for additional types of clock.

What to do

- Listen to the clocks working and discuss their different sounds.
- Make the sounds of different clocks:
    a deep, slow tick-tock for the grandfather clock
    a whispered tick-tock for a watch
    a chime – tinkling or booming
    a harsh ding-a-ling for the alarm clock.
- Hold up one picture or real clock. Children start making the appropriate sound effect.
- Change to another picture or clock and the children change their sound effect to match.

Tip

Don't stay on any one for too long, keep things moving.

Tip

Use this popular nursery rhyme to inspire artwork and interactive displays with clocks.

Activity 2

Aims and objectives

- Tuning into sounds we can make.
- Learning to keep in time.

What to do

- Sing or recite the rhyme, making sure all the children know the words and actions.
- Tick-tock uses two beats. Help the children clap two beats.
- They can experiment with clapping, or slapping thighs, clicking fingers, tapping knees, etc. as they say the 'tick-tock, tick-tock'.
- Now ask the children to keep the beat going while saying the words 'tick-tock', as the adult says the rhyme.
- Can the children keep the beat going?
- If there are two adults available divide the children into two groups, with an adult each. One group says the rhyme and the other keeps the beat going.

Tip

Add some musical instruments suitable for representing a clock ticking. What about when the clock chimes one!

Activity 3

Aims and objectives

- To enlarge their vocabulary.
- Learning to use positional language.

Preparation

- Display a picture or model of a tall clock.
- You will need a finger puppet mouse.

What to do

- The adult moves the mouse around a picture or model of a tall clock.
- Children call out where the mouse is:

  on top

  at the bottom

  going up

  at the side

  going down

  near the numbers

  behind the clock.

Tip

Children can make a clock from boxes, and their own finger puppet mouse from fabric scraps or the fingers cut off old gloves, with features stuck on.

Activity 4

Aims and objectives

- Talking about rhythm and rhyme.
- Learning to complete sentences using rhyming words.

What to do

- Ask the children if the mouse comes out when the clock strikes two, or three or four?
- Repeat the rhyme together but stop when you get to '. . . the clock struck . . .' and add a different number. What might the mouse do? Help the children invent new verses, e.g.

The clock struck two: the mouse said 'Boo!'

mouse lost his shoe

The clock struck three: mouse hurt his knee

the mouse said 'Wheee!'

The clock struck four: mouse ran out the door

he fell to the floor

The clock struck five: the mouse can jive

the mouse can drive.

Activity 5

Aims and objectives

- Talking about alliteration.
- Learning how different sounds are articulated.

What to do

- Help the children make up new nonsense rhymes for the first line of this rhyme.
- First talk with the children about the initial sounds of the three words 'Hickory dickory dock'.
- Focus on the second two words that start with the same sound. (Adults will also notice that the first two words rhyme.)
  Make up a few examples together, e.g.

  Tickory wickory wock
  Fickory pickory pock
  Bickory lickory lock.

- Once the pattern is established, try saying the first two words of this pattern yourself and letting the children supply the final word.

Tip

Keep this fun – simply encourage children to copy the pattern of the words.

Activity 6

Aims and objectives

- Listening and remembering rhythm and rhyme.
- Learning to listen to and be aware of rhyming strings.

What to do

- Tell the children that the mouse has run up the clock so many times he fancies a change. Where might he run up next?

- Think of some words beginning with /d/ that could be used to replace the word 'dock' – one-syllable words. You could even try making up some new words, e.g.

    Dare
    Do
    Dar
    Dan

- Now take some of these words and think up a rhyming place for the mouse to run up, e.g.

    Hickory dickory dare, the mouse ran up the chair
    Hickory dickory do, the mouse ran up the shoe
    Hickory dickory dar, the mouse ran up the car
    Hickory dickory dan, the mouse ran up the pan.

Activity 7

Aims and objectives

- Tuning into rhythm and rhyme.
- Learning to repeat a rhyming string.

What to do

- Help the children think of lots of words that rhyme with 'clock', e.g.

    dock
    sock
    lock
    shock
    choc
    frock
    hock
    knock.

- Include made-up words.

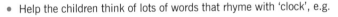

- Now play a memory game.

  Child One says, 'On my shelf I have a clock.'

  Child Two says, 'On my shelf I have a clock and a . . .'
- Continue round the group until you run out of words or memory!

Activity 8

Aims and objectives

- Tuning into rhythm and rhyme.
- Learning to experience and enjoy rhythm and rhyme.

Preparation

- You will need two stuffed toys – a mouse and a pig.

What to do

- There's a second less well-known verse to this rhyme

  Hickory dickory dare

  The pig flew in the air

  The man in brown

  Soon brought him down

  Hickory dickory dare.
- Ask the children what animal is in this verse?
- Say the rhyme together. Think of some actions for this verse.
- The children can take turns to say either of the verses to the rest of the group.
- Show the two stuffed toys – a pig and a mouse.
- Hold up one of the toys and ask the children to recite the appropriate verse.
- Let a child come to the front, and choose the verse by holding up one of the toys.

Activity 9

Aims and objectives

- Talking about rhythm and rhyme.
- Learning to complete sentences using rhyming words.

What to do

- Try adapting the lines, 'The man in brown / Soon brought him down.'
- Think of some other words that rhyme with brown, e.g.

    town
    crown

- Now re-create the two lines, e.g.

    The man in brown / Took him to town
    The man in brown / Gave him a crown.

    Repeat this with other colours, e.g.

    The man in blue / Soon saw him too
    The man in blue / Shouts 'boo, hoo, hoo'
    The man in red / Got out of bed
    The man in red / Then called him Fred
    The man in black / Soon brought him back
    The man in black / Gave him the sack
    The man in pink / Soon gave a wink.

Tip

Have a collection of scraps of fabric in plain colours. Put these in a bag or box. A child could choose one – unseen – and holds it up as the prompt for the next verse.

Other rhymes about pigs and mice for you to share with the children

'Three blind mice'
'Three little mice sat down to spin'
'This little piggy went to market'
'Tom, Tom the piper's son'.

'Miss Polly had a dolly'

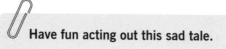

Have fun acting out this sad tale.

Resources

Doll, two telephones, a doctor's bag and hat, pen and notepad (Activities 1 & 4)

Tip

Include these activities during a theme about families or babies.

Activity 1

Aims and objectives

- Tuning into sounds we can make.
- Learning to join in with words and actions in songs.

Preparation

- Set out your props:
    a doll
    two telephones
    a bag
    a hat
    pen and notepad.

What to do

- Once the children are familiar with the words of the rhyme introduce some props.
- Choose two children to take the parts of Polly and the doctor.
- Let them examine the props and talk about when they will use them.
- As the children repeat the rhyme help the two actors to use the props to match the words, e.g.

'He wrote on a paper for a pill, pill, pill.' – the doctor uses the pen and notepad.

- Choose two more children to have a turn.

Activity 2

Aims and objectives

- Listening and remembering rhythm and rhyme.
- Learning to be aware of words that rhyme.

What to do

- Choose a child's name from the group, and say the rhyme using their name instead of 'Polly', e.g.
  Miss Sarah had a dolly

- Enjoy this using other children's names too.
- Then talk with the children about why the name 'Polly' has been used in this rhyme.
- Can they hear that Polly rhymes with dolly?
- Ask what other name might have worked just as well to fit the rhyme with 'dolly'? e.g.
  Miss Molly
  Miss Holly
  Miss Jolly
  Miss Wally.
- Try saying the rhyme with a new rhyming name.

Tip

Try 'Mr Freddy had a teddy' for a male version of this rhyme!

Activity 3

Aims and objectives

- Listening and remembering rhymes.
- Learning to be aware of words that rhyme.

What to do

- Say the rhyme, pausing before the rhyming word so that the children can put this in.
- This is particularly obvious in the lines with the three repeats in the first and last verses.
- Use the words from the rhyme and ask which word in the rhyme rhymes with – sick?
- The children answer – 'quick'.
- Now try – hat –' rat-a-tat-tat'.
- Continue with:
    head – 'bed'
    pill – 'bill'
    Polly – 'dolly'.

Tip

Extend this game to think of any other words that rhyme with these words.

Activity 4

Aims and objectives

- Talking about voice sounds.
- Learning to talk about different voice and speech sounds they hear or make.

Preparation

- Set out your props:
    a doll   a hat
    two telephones   pen and notepad.
    a bag

What to do

- Dress two children as the characters Miss Polly and the doctor.
- Use two telephones to recreate the conversation between them.

- Ask Polly to describe what's wrong with the dolly, and what she has already done for her.
- Ask the doctor to ask questions to find out more.

- Talk with the children about different voices.
- Is Miss Polly an old lady or a little girl?
- Miss Polly is very upset so she may be sobbing or speaking very quickly.
- Is the doctor a man or a woman?

Try to have the conversation in lots of different voices.

Tip

After this activity place the props in the role play area. Children may recreate the story for themselves.

Other rhymes about babies for you to share with the children

'Miss Lucy had a baby'
'Rock-a-bye baby'
'Bye baby bunting'
'Hush little baby'
'Pat-a-cake, pat-a-cake baker's man'.

'Incy wincy spider'

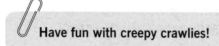

Have fun with creepy crawlies!

Resources

- Large watering can and toy spider (Activities 1 & 3)
- Selection of percussion instruments (Activity 3)
- Tambourine (Activity 4)

Tip

An ideal starting point for your work on mini-beasts.

Activity 1

Aims and objectives

- Tuning into sounds we can make.
- Learning to join in with words and actions in songs.

Preparation

- Set out a toy spider and a large watering can.

What to do

- Show the children the watering can.
- Talk about how to hold the handle and tip the can so the water comes out of the spout.
- Now show the children the spider.
- Can they guess which rhyme you are going to say?
- Recite the rhyme while you move the spider up and down the spout.
- Now the children can take turns to move the spider on the watering can as they say the rhyme.

- Then the children can take it in turns to come and move the spider
  according to your instructions:
  - up the spout
  - down the spout
  - over the top of the watering can
  - behind the watering can
  - round the spout
  - into the watering can.

Tip

Make your own spiders with black fur fabric and pipe cleaners, using sequins for
sparkly eyes.

Activity 2

Aims and objectives

- Talking about rhythm and rhyme.
- Learning to create their own rhymes.

What to do

- Think of a new last name for Incy.
- But remember it must rhyme! e.g.
    Incy mincy
    Incy tincy
    Incy chincy
    Incy kincy
    Incy dincy.
- Try saying the rhyme with these new names.
- Children could take it in turns to stand up and say the rhyme with their own choice of silly name for the spider.

Tip

If you have made your own spiders, give them each a name rhyming with Incy.

Activity 3

Aims and objectives

- Talking about instrumental sounds.
- Learning to use sound in imaginative ways.

Preparation

- Have a selection of instruments ready from which the children can choose.

What to do

- Let the children choose instruments or music-makers to create sound effects for the rhyme.
- Try:
    - a triangle for the spider
    - a shaker or rain-maker for the rain
    - a tambourine for the sun.
- Allow time for the children to experiment with these to find the best sound effect they can.

- Divide the group of children into three, each group concentrating on one of these:
  - playing the instruments
  - saying the words
  - acting out the rhyme with the toy spider and watering can.
- Take it in turns to do each part.

Activity 4

Aims and objectives

- Tuning into instrumental sounds.
- Learning to respond to musical sounds.

Preparation

- Use a tambourine.
- You'll need lots of room for this – or probably best to aim for a nice day when you can all go outside.

What to do

- Everyone can be a spider.
- The children say the rhyme as they move around on all fours as if they were spiders.
- When you reach the line about the rain, shake the tambourine
  - the children flop down flat on the ground.
- When you reach the line about the sun, tap the tambourine
  - the children sit up, make a sun-burst with their arms and smile.
- Once the children are familiar with the actions let them move freely as spiders, and then the adult plays one of the two sounds effects – rain or sun. The children respond with the chosen action. Who is listening well?

Other rhymes about mini-beasts to share with the children

'Ladybird, ladybird fly away home'
'Little Miss Muffet'.

'Mary had a little lamb'

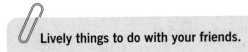

Lively things to do with your friends.

Resources

- Collection of toy farm animals and a bag (Activity 3)
- Toy lamb and ribbon tied as a bow (Activity 4)

Tip

These activities would be a useful addition to your work on pets or farm animals.

Activity 1

Aims and objectives

- Tuning into sounds we can make.
- Learning to join in with words and actions in songs.

What to do

- Learn the rhyme and practise saying it, keeping the rhythm.
- Play a follow-the-leader game.
- The children form pairs; the leader is 'Mary', the follower is the 'lamb'.
- They move around the room, or outdoor spaces, saying the rhyme as they go.
- Encourage the leader to change speed and direction, walk on tiptoe, stretch up tall or crouch down low.
- They could take it in turns to play these roles.

Activity 2

Aims and objectives

- Tuning into rhythm and rhyme.
- Learning to be aware of rhythm and rhyme in speech.

What to do

- Change the name of the child in the rhyme.
- Try choosing a child's name from the class.
- Say it with the new name. Does this name keep the rhythm going?
- Has it got two beats like 'Mary'?
- Clap while saying the name to demonstrate this.
- Change the animal that follows Mary. Try lots of different ones as suggested by the children.
- Check to see if the rhythm is maintained – you only need one beat for the animal.
- Put these two changes together to make some new rhymes. You may want to change 'fleece' to 'fur' or 'hair' or 'coat'. Let the children decide.
- Say your new rhymes together or let individual children show off their speaking skills, e.g.

  Lily had a little mouse / Its coat was white as snow
  Jamie had a little cat / Its fur was white as snow
  Ella had a little dog / Its hair was white as snow.

Tip

Each child can try saying the rhyme with their own name.

Activity 3

Aims and objectives

- Listening and remembering oral blending and segmenting.
- Learning to segment words into phonemes.

Preparation

- Put a collection of animals from your farm or zoo sets into a bag.
- The animal names need to be easy to segment.
- Try:
  d-o-g
  c-a-t
  h-or-se
  b-ear

sh-ee-p
f-o-x
p-i-g
r-a-t
m-ou-se.

Tip

Avoid any animal names that have two consecutive consonants that make individual sounds as in '**sn**ake' or '**z**ebra'. Young children find it too hard to separate these out.

What to do

- A child reaches in, chooses one animal at random and holds it tight within the bag.
- The child now segments its name.
- The others work out which animal it is by blending the sounds.
- Can they guess the animal?
- You may need to demonstrate this a few times first.

Activity 4

Aims and objectives

- Tuning into rhythm and rhyme.
- Learning to recognise that some words rhyme.

Preparation

- Collect a toy lamb and a ribbon tied in a bow.

What to do

- The children sit in a circle.
- Show them the toy lamb.
- Ask the children to think of words that rhyme with lamb.

- The lamb is passed around. When each child holds it they say a word that rhymes with **lamb**, e.g.
  ham
  jam
  ram
  wham
  yam
  Sam
- Or even some made up words: fam, tam, cam.
- Now repeat the activity with a ribbon tied in a **bow**, e.g.
  go
  slow
  show
  foe
  toe
  row
  sew
  throw
  snow
  blow.

Tip

Collecting the rhyming words before playing the game will help those children who find it tricky to think of words.

Activity 5

Aims and objectives

- Listening and remembering voice sounds.
- Learning to listen for a target word and respond.

Preparation

- Use a large outdoor space.

What to do

Decide on two actions or poses, one to represent Mary and one to represent the lamb, e.g.

Mary – a star jump

Lamb – down on all fours.

- The children dance around freely.
- The adult calls out 'Mary' or 'lamb'.
- The children stop their dancing and perform the action or take up the pose for that target word.

Tip

Play a percussion instrument or taped music as the children dance.

Other rhymes about children that you can share

'Polly put the kettle on'

'Lucy Locket lost her pocket'

'Little Jack Horner'

'Mary, Mary quite contrary'.

'Humpty Dumpty'

 It's all excitement even when things go wrong!

Resources

- A small bell or other quiet musical instrument (Activity 5)

Tip

Use these activities to add another dimension to your work on people who help us.

Activity 1

Aims and objectives

- Listening and remembering sounds we can make.
- Learning to create sounds for stories.

What to do

- Practise saying the rhyme.
- Ask the children to think up some sound effects for each line.
- Try:
    crack!
    crash!
    gallop
    sigh.
- How can we make these noises? With our own voices or bodies? Or with music-makers?
- Whichever version you decide on, spend time letting the children experiment until you are all happy with the sound effects.
- Now say the rhyme with sound effects. Half the group speaking, half of them providing the sound accompaniment.

Activity 2

Aims and objectives

- Tuning into rhythm and rhyme.
- Learning to experience and enjoy rhythm and rhyme.

Preparation

- A large space – outdoors would be ideal for this activity.

What to do

- Divide the children into two groups to act out the rhyme.
- Group One: hold hands and form a large egg shape or oval as one enormous Humpty.
- Group Two: kneel in a line to make a wall.
- Explain how each group moves:

Humpty Dumpty sat on a wall	(Group One stand near Group Two)
Humpty Dumpty had a great fall	(Group One drop to the ground in their shape)
All the king's horses and all the king's men	(Group Two children now stand and gallop around the fallen Humpty)
Couldn't put Humpty together again	(Group Two stop, shake heads and sigh).

- Perform the rhyme again with different children in each group.

Variation

- Try each child doing his own individual actions.
- Start with everyone as Humpty Dumpty.
- Say the rhyme and show the children the actions.
    Line 1: Stand up with arms clasped in front to look like a big tummy
    Line 2: Fall down flat
    Line 3: Gallop around
    Line 4: Hands on hips and shake head.

Activity 3

Aims and objectives

- Tuning into rhythm and rhyme.
- Learning to understand a pattern of syllables.

What to do

- Say the two words 'Humpty', 'Dumpty'.
- Clap in time to the speech.
- There are two beats per name, each one representing one syllable: Hump-ty and Dump-ty.
- Does anyone else in the group have a name with the same number of beats? e.g.
    Lily
    Freddie
    Joseph
    Sarah.
- Now have a go at clapping this rhythm through the whole rhyme.
- Try tapping alternate knees to emphasise the rhythm.

Activity 4

Aims and objectives

- Tuning into rhythm and rhyme.
- Learning to experience and enjoy rhythm and rhyme.

What to do

- Let the children enjoy the sounds of nonsense words as you make up new names for Humpty, e.g.
    Lumpty Pumpty
    Shrumpty Wumpty
    Rumpty Tumpty.
- The children can now enjoy reciting the rhyme with these new nonsense names.

Tip

A quick activity for when you need to fill a few spare moments.

Activity 5

Aims and objectives

- Listening and remembering rhythm and rhyme.
- Learning to be aware of words that rhyme.

Preparation

- You will need a small bell or other quiet musical instrument.

What to do

- Help the children to hear the words that rhyme as you say the whole rhyme together.
- Establish that the rhyming words are in pairs:
    wall/fall
    men/again.
- Tell the children you will ring the bell on the first word and they must clap on the rhyming word.
- Say the rhyme together.
    On 'wall' the adult rings the bell (This alerts the children to the rhyme.)
    On 'fall' the children clap (This shows that they have recognised the rhyme.)
    And again,
    On 'men' the adult rings the bell
    On 'again' the children clap.
- The children could then take it in turns to ring the bell.
- Or perhaps they would like to test the adult?
- The children clap the first word of each pair, the adult responds on the second word.

Tip

This activity could be adapted to any other rhyme.

Activity 6

Aims and *objectives*

- Talking about rhythm and rhyme.
- Learning to complete sentences using rhyming words.

What to do

- Ask the children to think about another place for Humpty to sit, e.g. on a chair.
- Say the first two lines of the rhyme using the word chair.
- Let the children realise that this doesn't work – that the rhyme isn't there any more.
- So now they will have to think up a new second line.
- Help the children think of words that rhyme with the chosen place, e.g.chair/air.
- Work with the children to find words that fit the rhythm and the rhyme, e.g.

Humpty Dumpty sat in a chair

Humpty Dumpty flew in the air.

Humpty Dumpty sat on a bus

Humpty Dumpty made a great fuss.

Humpty Dumpty sat on his bed

Humpty Dumpty fell on his head.

- If you want to complete the rhyme keeping some sense to the story of Humpty Dumpty an adult will need to provide an alternative last line, e.g.

Humpty Dumpty sat on a chair

Humpty Dumpty flew in the air

All the king's soldiers

And all the king's men

Couldn't get Humpty down here again.

    bus/fuss/ Couldn't get Humpty calmed down again.

    bed/head/ Couldn't get Humpty upright again.

Tip

Think of some possible rhymes in advance.

Activity 7

Aims and objectives

- Tuning into sounds we can make.
- Learning to recreate sounds with a variety of different rhythms, speed and volume.

What to do

- Say the rhyme through.
- Now say it very quickly.
- And then very slowly.
- Try saying it loud.
- Try whispering it.
- Once the children are able to do this spend some time working out hand signs to represent these different speeds and volume.
- The children start the rhyme in their normal voices, the adult shows one of the signs and the children have to change their pace or their volume accordingly.

Other rhymes about accidents to share with the children

'Jack and Jill'
'London's burning'
'Ding dong bell'
'Little Bo-Peep'.

. . . and any other rhyme

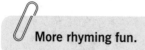 **More rhyming fun.**

Resources

- Toy lamb, soldier, mouse and spider (Activity 1)
- Rain-maker and bell (Activity 3)
- Number cards – 2, 3, 4 and taped music (Activity 4)

Tip

Try these when your children have built up a repertoire of rhymes.

Activity 1

Aims and objectives

- Tuning into rhythm and rhyme.
- Learning to understand the pattern of syllables.

Preparation

- You will need a toy lamb, soldier, mouse and spider.

What to do

- Ask the children to say which toy represents each nursery rhyme, e.g.
  lamb: 'Mary had a little lamb'
  soldier: 'Humpty Dumpty'
  mouse: 'Hickory dickory dock'
  spider: 'Incy Wincy spider'.
- Choose two of these toys and place them where everyone can see them.
- Make sure everyone knows which two rhymes they represent.
- Now clap the rhythm for one of their rhymes.
- Can the children identify which one it is?
- If the children find this easy try three toys to choose from.

Activity 2

Aims and objectives

- Listening and remembering voice sounds.
- Learning to recognise and identify different voices.

What to do

- One child comes to the adult and hides their eyes.
- Another child in the group is chosen – silently, so the first child doesn't know who it is!
- This child then says a rhyme.
- Without peeping the first child has to listen carefully.
- Can they recognise the voice? Can they guess who is saying the rhyme?

Tip

Try this with the children disguising their voices for even more fun.

Activity 3

Aims and objectives

- Listening and remembering sounds we can make.
- Learning to remember patterns of sounds.

Preparation

- You will need a bell and the rain-maker instrument.

What to do

- Make a sound effect with your voice or one of the instruments. Can the children guess the rhyme it is from, e.g.
  - tick-tock = 'Hickory dickory dock'
  - rain = 'Incy wincy spider'
  - baa, baa = 'Mary had a little lamb'
  - baby crying = 'Miss Polly had a dolly'
  - ring a bell= 'Ding dong bell'.

- If the children find this easy, use sound effects to create a sequence of sounds for any rhyme.
- Make them up together, e.g.
    crash, hooves galloping, sigh = 'Humpty Dumpty'
    baby crying, telephone ringing = 'Miss Polly had a dolly'.

Now play a sequence of sounds and ask the children which rhyme is this?

Activity 4

Aims and objectives

- Talking about oral blending and segmenting.
- Learning to identify the number of phonemes in a given simple word.

Preparation

- You will need three cards showing the numbers or symbols for 2, 3, 4.
- A large space and some taped music for dancing.
- Position the numbers 2, 3 and 4 in various corners of the room or grounds.

Tip

Make sure the children know how to count the phonemes or individual sounds on their fingers before playing this game.

What to do

- The children dance around saying or singing one of their favourite rhymes.
- The adult signals them to stop – if you have a music tape this is easier to do.
- The adult now segments one word linked to a nursery rhyme. The children have to count the phonemes and go to the appropriate number. Try:
    l-a-mb
    t-i-ck

m-e-n
r-ai-n
p-i-g
h-or-se
s-u-n
(all have three phonemes)
p-o-ll-y
l-i-tt-le
w-e-n-t
(have four phonemes)
g-o
ou-t
(have two phonemes).

Part 3
Problem solving, reasoning and numeracy

Chapter 5
Boxes

All of these problem solving, reasoning and numeracy activities revolve around boxes and their many functions. They form an introduction to your work on shape and space, as well as providing you with numerous opportunities to think about sounds, rhymes, alliteration and developing the children's mathematical vocabulary.

New shoes

Activities for when you have a shoe shop in your role play area.

Resources

- A selection of different types of shoes (Activities 1 & 2)
- Shoe boxes and soft toys (dolls, teddies, etc.) (Activity 2)
- Three pairs of shoes that make different sounds, a blanket or piece of fabric to form a screen (Activity 3)

Tip

Larger shoe stores will be happy to let you have unused shoe boxes if you give them advance warning.

Activity 1

Aims and objectives

- Tuning into alliteration.
- Learning to make up alliterative phrases.

Preparation

- Have a collection of different kinds of shoes.

What to do

- Let the children have some time to handle the shoes.
- Then, sit in a circle with the shoes in the middle.
- One at a time, children can come into the middle and choose a pair of shoes. What sort of shoes are they? Help the children identify them, e.g.
  sandals
  slippers

wellies
boots
flip-flops
mules
shoes
trainers.

- Taking each type in turn find some words that start with the same sound to describe them, e.g.

  silver, smart, soft . . . sandals/slippers
  warm, white, wet . . . wellies
  blue, brown, beautiful . . . boots
  fancy, flat, flowery . . . flip-flops
  marvellous, mauve . . . mules
  shiny, showy . . . shoes
  tatty, terrific . . . trainers.

- Now turn some of these ideas into phrases.
- Be ready with some examples to help the children understand what you want them to do, e.g.

  Mummy is wearing her marvellous mules.
  Fancy wearing flip-flops on a frosty Friday.
  Sharon wore her shiny shoes going to the shops.

Activity 2

Aims and objectives

- Listening and remembering alliteration.
- Learning to match sounds to objects.

Preparation

- Have a selection of different kinds of footwear.
- Stand each pair in a separate shoe box.
- A selection of toys – dolls, teddies or other soft toys.

What to do

- Show the children the different shoes and make sure that they can name them.
- Take one of the dolls, soft toys or teddies.
- Tell the children what the toy is called.
- Explain to the children that it can only wear shoes that start with the same sound as its name.
- Children suggest which shoes the toy might wear.
- When all are agreed, one of the children places the toy in the box with the appropriate shoes, e.g.
  - Sam wears sandals
  - William wears wellies.

Tip

Have more shoes than dolls so that there is always a choice for the children to make, even for the last doll.

Variation

- Change the rule of the game so that the toys can only wear shoes that don't have the same sound as their name, e.g.
  - Tom can't wear trainers – but he could wear wellies or slippers
  - Ben can't wear boots – but he could wear sandals or flip-flops.

Activity 3

Aims and objectives

- Tuning into environmental sounds.
- Learning to discriminate between sounds.

Preparation

- You will need three pairs of shoes. They need to make distinctive and different sounds, e.g.
  - mules or flip-flops
  - wellies, slippers or plimsolls
  - outdoor shoes or heeled shoes.

What to do

- Show the three pairs of shoes to the children and identify them.
- Two children or adults can hold up a blanket or large piece of fabric to make a curtain – make sure it's touching the floor!
- One child goes behind, chooses one pair of shoes, puts them on and walks in them.
- Can the others identify which pair of shoes it is?
- Lift the 'curtain' to reveal whether they guessed correctly or not.

Tip

Find a hard surface to walk on.

Activity 4

Aims and objectives

- Tuning into sounds we can make.
- Learning to join in with words and actions in songs.

What to do

- There are plenty of action rhymes that involve shoes or walking.
- Encourage the children to join in with the words.
- Teach them the actions and have lots of fun.
- You could try:
  'One, two, buckle my shoe'
  'Can you walk on tiptoe?'
  'Slowly, slowly walks my granddad'.

Postbox

 Have lots of fun posting letters!

Resources

- Postbox, some large and small envelopes and two instruments with contrasting sounds (Activity 1)
- Large cardboard box (or lots of tubes), strong scissors, red paint (Activity 2)
- Small soft parcel (Activity 3)
- Children's own drawings in envelopes and a postbox (Activity 4)
- Picture of people in uniform or at work (Activity 5)
- Two boxes with posting holes, a picture of a dog, and a picture of a cat. A selection of other pictures that start with /d/ and /k/ sounds (Activity 7)

Tip

Activities to use with the postbox in the classroom – postboxes are not just for Christmas!

Activity 1

Aims and objectives

- Talking about instrumental sounds.
- Learning to match sounds to instruments.

Preparation

- Your postbox.
- A selection of 'letters' in large and small envelopes.
- Two instruments placed out of sight of the children.

What to do

- Provide a small group of children with a pile of letters waiting to be posted.
- Ensure there are a mixture of large envelopes and small ones.

- Have two contrasting musical instruments, e.g. a chime bar and a drum.
- Place these out of sight after you have demonstrated the two different sounds that they make.
- Tell the children they must listen carefully to find out which type of letter to post.
- Tell the children when they hear the drum they must find a large letter and when they hear the chime bar they need to find a small one.
- Choose a child to take the first turn.
- Hit the drum – encourage them to post a large letter.
- Once the children have the idea, use the instruments to indicate that two or three letters need posting at once, e.g. drum, drum, chime bar.
- Can the child find the correct letters to post?
- Now let a child play the instruction for another child to post the letter.

Variation

- Change the game by sorting brown and white envelopes to a matching sound.

Activity 2

Aims and objectives

- To develop vocabulary.
- Learning to talk about shapes in the environment.

Preparation

- You will need a large cardboard box, some strong scissors and red paint.
- Take the children out to see a postbox and discuss its size and shape.
- Have the children seen other postboxes that are different?

What to do

- Children will enjoy making a postbox from a large cardboard box.
- While they are working, talk about the shape of the box.

How many corners?

How many flat faces?

What flat shape are they painting?

Introduce the name 'cuboid'.

- Let the children spot other cuboids around the classroom, outside and at home.
- You may prefer to let the children make small individual postboxes using cardboard tubes.
- Talk about the basic solid shape.
- Introduce the name 'cylinder'.
- Show them that it is made from one flat rectangle that has been rolled into a cylinder.
- What shape do we need to make a top and a base for the postbox?

Tip

Have the children noticed how many words begin in the same way? E.g. postman . . . post office . . . post box . . . post van.

How many words can they think of that begin with 'police'?

Activity 3

Aims and objectives

- Tuning into sounds we can make.
- Learning to join in with words and actions.

Preparation

- You will need a small, soft parcel that the children can easily hold, for the packet.
- Make a circle and sit down.

What to do

- Teach the children this adapted version of the traditional rhyme:

  Lucy Lockett went to post a packet
  But on the way she dropped it
  Now someone else has picked it up
  And put it in their pocket.

- Choose a child to be Lucy Lockett (or Lenny Lockett)
- As the children sing, the child playing Lucy Lockett walks around the outside of the circle.
- She drops the small packet behind another child who is sitting in the circle.
- This child picks up the packet and runs around the circle after Lucy Lockett.
- The first child runs all the way round the circle and sits down in the empty space.
- Repeat as many times as you wish or until everyone has had a turn.

Activity 4

Aims and objectives

- Tuning into oral blending and segmenting.
- Learning to blend phonemes into words.

Preparation

- The children draw pictures of their own choice and put the drawings into envelopes.
- Let them choose another child from the class to send their picture to.
- Then the adult prints that child's name on the envelope.
- All the letters are then posted into your postbox.

What to do

- Sit in a circle around the postbox.
- Tell the children it's time to empty the postbox and deliver the letters.

- Take an envelope out and say, 'This one's for..../s/.../a/.../s/.../k/.../i/.../a/.'
- The children must try to blend the phonemes together and work out who the letter is for.
- Children can take turns to wear the postman's uniform when they deliver the letters.

Variation

If this game is too difficult for the children try this simpler variation:

- Choose three soft toys with simple names that are easy to segment, e.g. Bob, Mog, Pat.
- The children decide which toy they want to send their picture to.
- Write one of the names on each envelope.
- Post them and then empty the box as before.
- Segment each name and see if the children can work out which toy the letter is for.

Tip

To make this a little harder try choosing three names that all begin with the same initial phoneme.

Activity 5

Aims and objectives

- Tuning into alliteration.
- Learning to make up alliterative phrases.

Preparation

- Prepare some pictures of people in uniform or as they do their jobs.

What to do

- Ask if the children all watched *Postman Pat* on the television.
- Tell them Postman Pat is a special name because Pat begins with the same sound as postman.

- Who can tell you what that sound is?
- Show the children one of the pictures, e.g. 'Here is a picture of a mmmmmm milkman . . .' 'Can anyone think of a special name for him?'
  Milkman Mikey
- Go through the pictures taking suggestions.
- Then turn the pictures face down and let the children take turns to choose one.
- If they can suggest a name that begins with the same sound they can keep the picture.
- Once they have the idea of the game, see who can collect the most.
- Ideas to use:
  Fireman Fred
  Nurse Norman
  Doctor Dora
  Policewoman Penny
  Gardener Gavin
  Mechanic Mandy
  Teacher Ted
  Builder Barbara
  Librarian Les
  Dentist Davina.

Tip

Try to include pictures of women and men in a variety of roles – challenge stereotypes!

Activity 6

Aims and objectives

- Tuning into environmental sounds.
- Learning to develop listening skills.

Preparation

- Place a tin that held sweets or biscuits inside your postbox. (No lid on the tin!)
- Have some plastic cubes ready.

What to do

- Tell the children they must listen and count to tell you how many 'letters' are being posted.
- When everyone is quiet, place the box and some cubes behind a screen so the children can't see your hands.
- Now slowly drop a small number of cubes into the container, one at a time.
- Encourage the children to count as you drop the cubes in.
- How many were there?
- Bring the box into view and count out the cubes together.
- Next time ask individual children to count the 'letters' dropping into the postbox.
- Let the children take turns dropping the cubes into the box behind the screen.

Activity 6

Aims and objectives

- Listening and remembering sounds we can make.
- Learning to create sounds for stories.

What to do

- Make up a story with the children about going to post a letter.
- Decide what the weather is like and how far away the postbox is; how will you dress?
- Will you walk, skip or run to the postbox?
- Make up some sounds and actions together to accompany the story, e.g.

One snowy morning I went out to post a letter. It was very cold so I put on my coat, hat and big boots. (*Huddle into your imaginary coat, rubbing your hands together saying brrrrr.*)

Outside the snowflakes were falling and it was difficult to walk in the deep snow. (*Make whispery sounds and wriggle your fingers to show the snow falling and stamp your feet slowly and heavily.*)

- On the way something happens, e.g.

  Suddenly you see some of your friends throwing snowballs so you stop and play. Now you can see the post van coming down the road so you must hurry or you'll miss the post. (*Huff and puff, slipping and sliding as you try to rush to the postbox.*)

- Decide on the ending of your story . . . Will you get there in time and hear the letter dropping into the box? Or will you fall over with a big crash!

Tip

Changing the weather helps children make different sound effects like running quickly through the raindrops. The weather can also help to suggest what might happen in the story – did I hear thunder?

Activity 7

Aims and objectives

- Listening and remembering alliteration.
- Learning to hear the difference in sounds at the beginning of words.

Preparation

- You will need two boxes with holes for letters to play this game.
- Put a picture of a dog on one and a cat on the other.
- Provide the children with a set of pictures to sort. These will begin with either /k/ or /d/ sounds.

What to do

- Sit in a circle with the two boxes at the front.
- Talk about the two pictures, and identify the animals and the sounds that their names start with.
- Tell the children that they are to post the pictures in the right box.
- If the picture begins with /d/ it goes in the dog's box, if it begins with /k/ it goes in the cat's box.

- Pick up a picture card and show the children.
- Ask them what it is and decide together what sound it begins with.
- Then choose a child to post it into the correct box.
- Useful pictures to use:
  /d/ – dress, dragon, drink, desk, dinosaur, duck, drum, donkey
  /k/ – camera, car, carrot, comb, clock, cracker, coat, kitten.
- Repeat the game with two different initial sounds. Remember to change the pictures on the posting boxes.

Tip

At the end of the game empty the boxes and ask individual children to name the picture – can they reproduce the initial sound clearly?

Take a large box . . .

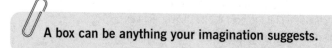

A box can be anything your imagination suggests.

Resources

- Four large boxes and doll's house furniture, and some small bears (Activities 1 & 2)
- *Peace at Last* by Jill Murphy (Activity 1)
- Recording of household noises (Activity 2)
- Set of identical large boxes, string (Activity 3)
- Large cardboard box (Activities 4 & 5)
- *Mr Gumpy's Motor Car* or *Mr Gumpy's Outing* by John Burningham (Activity 4)
- Musical instruments in a basket (Activity 5)

Tip

Collect big boxes whenever they are available, and collapse them down for storage. Use masking tape when you make them back into boxes as you can paint or stick over it.

Activity 1

Aims and objectives

- Tuning into environmental sounds.
- Learning to be aware of sounds around them.

Preparation

- Make a large box, or four smaller ones fixed together, into a house, with an open frontage.
- Use doll's house furniture or the children's own cardboard box constructions to make furniture – you will need a bed.
- Have your copy of *Peace at Last* by Jill Murphy ready.
- Choose some small bears that will fit into your house.

What to do

- Read the story *Peace at Last* by Jill Murphy.
- Retell it in your own words using the pictures as prompts.
- Choose children to move the bears around in the house as the story goes along.
- Discuss the sounds that the bear hears.
- Let the children work out how to make these noises.
- Children can add these sound effects to the story as you tell it.

Activity 2

Aims and objectives

- Tuning into environmental sounds.
- Learning to be aware of sounds around them.

Preparation

- Your house and bears as in Activity 1.
- Prepare a recording of sounds you might hear around the home, e.g.
    Kitchen: washing machine, microwave, kettle
    Garden: lawn mower, dog, birds
    Bathroom: taps, toilet flushing, splashing
    Living areas: television, vacuum cleaner, computer games.

What to do

- Sit in a circle around the house and the bears.
- Play one of the sounds.
- Can the children identify the sound?
- Can they work out in which room in the house they are most likely to hear this sound?
- Choose a child to put the bear in the appropriate part of the house.
- Continue playing sounds for the children to identify.
- Take turns moving the bears into the appropriate rooms.

Activity 3

Aims and objectives

- Tuning into environmental sounds.
- Learning to describe sounds.

Preparation

- Use a number of identical cardboard boxes to make a train.
- Have the tops open, and join them together with string.
- This should be big enough to hold dolls and teddies.

Tip

If you can get some very large boxes, make it outside and let the children 'ride' in it.

What to do

- Encourage the children to make sound effects as they play with the train.

- Talk about the different noises that the train can make.
  Why is it sometimes called a 'choo-choo'?
  Why is it sometimes called a 'puffer train'?
- Sing 'Puffer train, puffer train, noisy little puffer train.'
- This includes the noises 'ff, ff, ff', 'sh, sh, sh' and 'ch, ch, ch'.

- Adapt the song 'She'll be coming round the mountain' adding 'choo-choo' at the end of lines one, two and four, e.g.

  She'll be coming round the mountain when she comes. Choo-choo!
  She'll be coming round the mountain when she comes. Choo-choo!
  She'll be coming round the mountain, coming round the mountain
  Coming round the mountain when she comes. Choo-choo!

- Sing as you move round in a long line. Match the words to your route!

  We'll be coming round the sand pit, when we come. Choo-choo!
  We'll be coming round the car mat
  We'll be coming past the office
  We'll be coming near the paintings, etc.

- Try reading the first four lines of Robert Louis Stephenson's rhyme 'From a railway carriage' to the children. Can they feel the rhythm of the train in the way this is written?

Activity 4

Aims and objectives

- Listening and remembering sounds we can make.
- Learning to distinguish between sounds.

Preparation

- Copies of either of the *Mr Gumpy's Motor Car*, or *Mr Gumpy's Outing* by John Burningham.
- Make a car or a boat from a very large box.

What to do

- Read your chosen book to the children.
- Look through the pictures for the children to work out which friends Mr Gumpy takes along with him on his journey.
- He takes two children, a rabbit, a cat, a dog, a pig, a sheep, some chickens, a calf and a goat.
- What noises might you hear?
- Think about one 'friend' at a time and work out a sound effect for that person or animal.
- Retell the story with the children adding the sound effects in the right places.
- Choose three children to sit in the car/boat.
- Show each child one animal picture from the story, and tell them that they are to make that sound when you tell them to. Don't let the other children know which picture you have seen!
- You say, 'In Mr Gumpy's motor car (boat) today he has' and then the three children make their sound effects at the same time!
- Can the others work out which three characters are in the car/boat?

Activity 5

Aims and objectives

- Tuning into instrumental sounds.
- Learning to develop awareness of the sounds made by different musical instruments.

Preparation

- Place a very large box so that the open end is facing away from the group of children.
- Have a basket containing a number of musical instruments near the opening.

What to do

- One child at a time sits in the box, chooses an instrument and plays it.
- Can the others guess what he has chosen?
- 'What's in the box?'
  Sam and a . . . drum
  Ellie and a . . . triangle
  Anji and a . . . castanet.

. . . and a teeny, tiny box

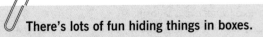

There's lots of fun hiding things in boxes.

Resources

- A set of identical boxes (Activities 1 & 2)
- Selection of everyday items that will fit into your boxes (Activity 1)
- Selection of small objects, most of which begin with the same sound (Activity 2)
- Six identical boxes (Activity 3)
- Sand, salt, rice, pasta, pebbles and gravel (Activity 3)

Tip

Look in the treasure chest section of Chapter 3, Pirates, for more ideas that could be adapted for use with small boxes.

Activity 1

Aims and objectives

- Listening and remembering sounds we can make.
- Learning to distinguish between sounds.

Preparation

- Place some everyday items into individual small cardboard boxes, e.g.
    a bunch of keys
    a small jigsaw
    a ball
    a book
    dried pasta
    a necklace
    some pieces of chalk or crayon
    a pair of socks.

Tip

Having a number of identical boxes would be helpful for these activities.

What to do

- Pick up one of the boxes, shake it gently.
- Can the children guess what is inside the box?
- Once some guesses have been made, let one of the children open the box and find out if anyone gave the right answer.
- That child can choose the next box and shake it for the others to guess.
- Be aware that if the children shake the boxes themselves they will get clues from the feel of the movement and the weight, so for best effect the one who guesses should not be the one who shakes!

Tip

Younger children may find it helpful if you show them the objects before they go in.

Activity 2

Aims and objectives

- Listening and remembering alliterative sounds.
- Learning to match sounds to objects.

Preparation

- Each child needs a box the same size and shape.
- Collect together some objects that all start with the same sound, but that are small enough to fit inside your boxes.
- Add a few extra items that don't start with this sound.

Tip

Let the children decorate their box with a variety of collage materials and paint. Do this a few days before you want to play this game.

What to do

- Lay out your selection of small objects – remember to have things that are smaller than the boxes.

- Most of these objects will begin with the same sound, but some will be different.
- Choose a sound that offers lots of small objects, e.g.
    button
    bead
    bean
    badge
    brooch
    blue (scraps of paper or fabric)
    band
    boat
    brick
    ball.
- The children hunt through the objects and find ones that start with a given sound.
- How many can you fit in your box?
- Count up the contents of each individual box and work out who has the most.
- Once the children understand this activity, they can be sent out around the setting to find other small objects that all begin with the same sound.

Activity 3

Aims and objectives

- Talking about environmental sounds.
- Learning to identify sounds that are similar.

Preparation

- You will need six boxes.
- Put one of these six items into each box and seal securely: sand, salt, rice, pasta, pebbles and gravel.

What to do

- The game involves pairing up the boxes with the sounds that are most alike.
- Children choose one box, shake it and listen. Now they test each of the other boxes and find the one that sounds most like their chosen box.
- Continue until all the boxes are paired up.
- They should end up with:
    sand and salt
    rice and pasta
    pebbles and gravel.
- Can they guess what is in each box?

Activity 4

Aims and objectives

- Tuning into sounds we can make.
- Learning to join in with words and actions in songs.

What to do

- *Fingers, Feet and Fun* by Delphine Evans contains a counting rhyme: '5 big crackers in a box'.
- There are sound effects and actions as you count down the numbers.

- Sing 'A-hunting we will go'.
- Two adults stand holding hands, with their arms raised.
- Children skip round in a circle, passing underneath the adults' arms.
- When you sing the line 'We'll catch a fox' the arms are lowered to 'catch' a child.
- On the words 'and put him in a box' the child who's been caught stands behind the adult who is 'inside' the circle of children and holds onto the adult.
- The rhyme starts again, and is repeated until there are three foxes in the box, when you let them free and start the game again.

My Cat Likes to Hide in Boxes by Eve Sutton

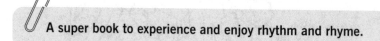

A super book to experience and enjoy rhythm and rhyme.

Resources

- *My Cat Likes to Hide in Boxes* by Eve Sutton (All activities)
- Large cardboard box (Activity 2)

Tip

A lovely book to read during a theme about pets. How many children have a pet cat?

Activity 1

Aims and objectives

- Tuning into rhythm and rhyme.
- Learning to experience and enjoy rhythm and rhyme.

Preparation

- Read the book *My Cat Likes to Hide in Boxes* by Eve Sutton to the children.
- Encourage them to join in with the repeating words 'my cat likes to hide in boxes'.

What to do

- Read the book again. As you do so, show the children the pictures to prompt them to recall the rhymes, e.g.
  You read: 'The cat from Norway . . .' (pause and show the picture)
  The children say: 'Got stuck in the doorway . . .'
- This text is accumulative, and gives an opportunity to practise reciting rhyming phrases.
- When the children are familiar with the book, choose pairs of children to say the words for the seven different cats.

- Sit them in the order they appear in the book.

- Read the story showing the picture to act as a prompt for each pair to recite their words.
- After each cat is introduced, the earlier cats repeat their rhyming phrases, e.g.
  - France
  - Spain, France
  - Norway, Spain, France

But everyone joins in with – 'My cat likes to hide in boxes!'
It's a bit like 'Old MacDonald had a farm'!

Tip

Give the children a picture or an item to remind them which cat they have chosen, e.g. a model plane or a policeman's hat.

Activity 2

Aims and objectives

- Listening and remembering environmental sounds.
- Learning to imitate sounds.

Preparation

- Have a large cardboard box, big enough for a child to get into.

What to do

- Show the children a large cardboard box.
- Do they think the cat could hide in it?

- What other pet animal might hide in there?
- Let a child hide in the box and make an animal sound for the others to guess – Is it a mouse? Or a dog? Or a frog?
- What other animals can they hide in the box?
- Take it in turns until everyone has had a go.

Activity 3

Aims and objectives

- Listening and remembering rhythm and rhyme.
- Learning to be aware of words that rhyme.

What to do

- When the children confidently know the rhyming phrases in the book, ask who can tell you the word from the book that rhymes with:
  France
  Spain
  Norway
  Greece
  Brazil
  Berlin
  Japan.
- Can anyone think of another rhyming word?
- You may need to start the ball rolling with a few suggestions.
  France: dance, prance, glance, chance, trance, advance
  Spain: plane, mane, pain, chain, lane, brain, train
  Norway: doorway, away, day, hay, may, say, pay
  Greece: police, niece, fleece, geese, grease, release
  Brazil: chill, pill, hill, until, will, still, bill
  Berlin: violin, Merlin, chin, pin, win, tin, thin
  Japan: fan, man, tan, ran, can, span, pan.
- Perhaps you can make up a new rhyming phrase for the children to enjoy, e.g.
  The cat from Berlin was awfully thin
  The cat from Norway went the wrong way.

Tip

It would be fun to let the children listen to some of the different languages mentioned in the book, or play some music associated with the countries.

Activity 4

Aims and objectives

- To develop vocabulary.
- Learning to use descriptive language correctly.

What to do

- What kinds of boxes do we see in the storybook?
- Let the children try to remember them, or show them the pictures and let them name the box shown, e.g. a wooden box, seed box, hat box, jewellery box, toy box.
- See how many other boxes you can think of, e.g.
    shoe box
    cereal box
    postbox
    book box
    chocolate box.
- Sit in a circle.
- One child comes into the middle and mimes using a box.
- Can the others can guess which one it is?

Activity 5

Aims and objectives

- Talking about alliteration.
- Learning to select a range of words that start with the same sound.

What to do

- The book ends by describing all the cats as clever.
- Emphasise the initial sound of the words *clever cats*.
- Ask the children to think of another word that begins with /k/ that can be used to describe cats, here are a few suggestions to use:
    cute
    kind
    cross
    careful
    cartoon
    comical
    crispy
    cream
    cuddly
    creepy
    cruel
    colourful
    clean.
- How many can you think of?

Tip

Suggest that the children bring a word from home that begins with /k/ and can be used to describe a cat.

Activity 6

Aims and objectives

- Listening and remembering oral blending and segmenting.
- Learning to listen to phonemes in words.

Preparation

- Have the book *My Cat Likes to Hide in Boxes* by Eve Sutton.

What to do

- Open the book at random.
- Tell the children you are going to say the place the cat is from.
- Who can identify where the cat is from?
- Now slowly segment the name into phonemes, e.g.
    n-or-w-ai.

- Be careful to separate the two consonants at the beginning of these words:
    F-r-a-n-s
    S-p-ai-n
    G-r-ee-s
    B-r-a-z-i-l.

- When they have guessed correctly, let the children make actions and sound effects as they join in with the words, e.g. waving a fan, playing the violin, sneezing, saluting, being very fat, flying an aeroplane.

Tip

This is an activity that needs an adult to do the segmenting. It is probably too hard for the children to sort out the consonant blends, f-r, g-r, etc.

Chapter 6
Explorers

During their problem solving, reasoning and numeracy development children need time to practise talking about mathematical problems as well as counting. The following activities, many focusing on stories and rhymes, present such opportunities while also extending children's language skills.

We're Going on a Bear Hunt
by Michael Rosen

A fantastic adventure story with super sound effects about a family of explorers who find a bear.

Resources

- *We're Going on a Bear Hunt* by Michael Rosen (All activities)
- Collage materials, paper and glue (Activitiy 2)
- Percussion instruments (Activity 3)

Aims and objectives

- Tuning into sounds we can make.
- Learning to join in with words and actions in songs.

Preparation

- Enjoy reading *We're Going on a Bear Hunt* by Michael Rosen.

What to do

- Once the children are familiar with the book, emphasise the rhythm of the chorus.
- Establish a regular beat by clapping your hands together then tapping your knees in a repeating pattern. Encourage the children to join in with the actions.
- Then introduce the words of the chorus as you clap your hands and tap your knees keeping a steady beat, e.g.

  We're . . . going . . . on . . . a . . . bear . . . hunt

  . . . clap . . . tap . . . clap . . . tap . . .

- At the words . . . *Uh-uh Grass* – spread hands in a querying way.
- Then indicate with hands – going over and going under and pushing through.

- Once the children are familiar with the actions for the chorus, introduce actions for each of the six obstacles in turn: grass, river, mud, forest, snowstorm and cave, e.g.
  - Show the children the illustration of the grass.
  - Speak the onomatopoeic words, *swishy, swashy*, in a way that represents the sound of moving long grass. Do this quietly at first and then growing louder – as indicted by the printed text.
- Now introduce a matching action, e.g. waving arms gently from side to side to mimic the effect of long wavy grass.
- Practise the words and actions for each of the six obstacles in the story.

Tip

Don't attempt the return journey now – save this for a later treat!

Activity 2

Aims and objectives

- Listening and remembering voice sounds.
- Learning to remember a sound sequence.

Preparation

- Enjoy reading *We're Going on a Bear Hunt* by Michael Rosen.
- Collage materials, paper and glue.

What to do

- Help the children create collage pictures of the six obstacles explored in the story.
- While they are working remind them of the words from the text, such as 'a deep cold river'.
- Display these pictures and see if they can remember the pattern of words for each one.
- Talk about which came first, second, third, fourth, etc.
- Display them in the correct order.

- When the children are fairly confident about the sound sequences for each picture encourage them to increase the volume as they repeat the words.
- Introduce the return journey saying it at a faster pace.
- Choose a child to point to each picture as it is reached during the journey.

Variation

- The children can vary the order of the pictures to make each journey different.

Tip

Are your children ready to notice that the print size increases with each repetition?

Activity 3

Aims and objectives

- Talking about instrumental sounds.
- Learning to express an opinion about different sounds.

Preparation

- Enjoy reading *We're Going on a Bear Hunt* by Michael Rosen.
- Have some percussion instruments available.

What to do

- Use the illustrations in the book or the pictures the children have created of the six obstacles explored on the journey.
- Select one of the pictures and ask the children to choose an instrument to represent it.
- Use both the description and the onomatopoeic words from the story to help the children make an appropriate choice.
- Let two or three children select and play the instruments they've chosen to represent the first picture.

- Encourage them to explain their choices.
- Then ask the other children which instrument they think is the most suitable for the conditions, e.g. a shaker will be nearer to the swishy swashy sounds of the long wavy grass than a drum!
- Repeat with other pictures and instruments.

Activity 4

Aims and objectives

- Listening and remembering sounds we can make.
- Learning to remember patterns of sounds.

Preparation

- Enjoy reading *We're Going on a Bear Hunt* by Michael Rosen.

What to do

- Remind the children of the obstacles the children meet in the story using the illustrations or pictures the children have created.
- Do the actions and sound-effect words for three places, e.g. mud, forest, cave.
- Can the children tell you what they are?
- Ask one child to decide on three places – but don't tell the others!
- The child then says the sound effects – using the words from the book if he can, e.g.

    Squelch, squerch, squelch, squerch, squelch, squerch
    Stumble trip, stumble trip, stumble trip
    Tiptoe, tiptoe, tiptoe.

- The other children have to guess where he is as he travels.
- If the child can then say the pattern in reverse, everyone gives them a clap!

Tip

The children might find it easier to do the actions along with the sounds.

Activity 5

Aims and objectives

- To engage with books.
- To make up a new story based on *We're Going on a Bear Hunt.*

Tip

Look out for the many opportunities to bring mathematical concepts – shape, number and size, etc into this work.

Preparation

- Enjoy reading *We're Going on a Bear Hunt* by Michael Rosen.

What to do

- Look at the original book and count how many people are going exploring.
- Ask the children questions about the characters:
  - Who are they? e.g. Is that daddy or an uncle or a big brother?
  - How old are the children? e.g. Has anyone got a baby brother about the same size / age as this baby?
- Ask the children:
  'If you were going on a bear hunt who would you take with you?'
- Ask children questions about the bear, e.g.
  - Does he live in the cave?
  - What does he eat?
  - Why do you think he chased after them?
- Ask the children, e.g.
  - If you were going out exploring what animal would you like to find?
- Make up a new story about going on a hunt for a different animal.
- Use the pattern and language of the published story.
- Then act out your story together.

Tip

Simplify your story by only travelling through three or four different places on your route.

Off we go!

There are lots opportunities for phonics when pretending to go exploring.

Resources

- A backpack (Activities 1 & 2)
- Two shakers, two drums, two bells, two tambourines (Activities 4 & 5)
- Toy binoculars – optional (Activities 6 & 7)

Tip

Make some toy binoculars with cardboard rolls and let the children go out exploring – look out for footprints and wild animals!

Activity 1

Aims and objectives

- Listening to and remembering about alliteration.
- Learning to suggest objects that start with the same sound.

Preparation

- Have a backpack containing things you might need when you go out exploring.

What to do

- Ask the children to guess what's inside the backpack.
- Reach inside and choose an object but don't pull it out.
- Tell them you will give them a clue – 'I'm taking something that begins with . . .', e.g.
  /k/ cup, camera, kettle
  /a/ apple

/t/ torch, towel
/b/ book, biscuit
/p/ pencil, paper
/s/ string, spoon
/d/ drink.

- The children guess.
- Then you show the object and they can see if they were right.
- Once they have the idea of the game, a child can take turns reaching into the bag and giving the initial sound clue to what he has selected.

Activity 2

Aims and objectives

- Tuning into oral blending and segmenting.
- Learning to blend phonemes into words.

Preparation

- Hide some things in the backpack that can be used for blending and segmenting.

What to do

- Tell the children you will give a different sort of clue this time

    'When I go exploring today I'm taking a . . . c – u – p.
    Who knows what I'm taking?'

- Good things to hide in the backpack for this activity:
    m-a-p
    t-or-ch
    kn-i-fe
    c-a-ke
    a-pp-le
    b-ow-l
    h-a-t
    p-e-n.

- When the children are familiar with the game and the items have all been taken out of the backpack ask the children to help you pack the things away again.

  'Who can find the c – u – p?'

- Select one child at a time to put the named item back in the bag.

Tip

Be careful not to include any names containing sounds with double consonants which would be too difficult to segment, e.g. drink.

Activity 3

Aims and objectives:

- Talking about alliteration.
- Learning to select a range of words that start with the same sound.

What to do

- Hold hands to form a circle and to the tune of 'Hickory dickory dock' sing:
  We're going exploring today
  We're going exploring today
  Off we go
  Off we go
  We're going to the ...forest ...today.
- Now tell the children that because you are going to the forest you can take with you anything that begins with /f/.
- Ask for suggestions, e.g.
    fish
    friends
    feathers
    football

fork

frog.

- Sing the song again but explore the jungle and ask for words that begin with /j/.
- Repeat again exploring the seaside and river or other places that fit in with your current theme.

Activity 4

Aims and objectives

- Listening and remembering instrumental sounds.
- Learning to remember and repeat a rhythm.

Preparation

- Select pairs of instruments, e.g. two shakers, two drums, two bells, two tambourines

What to do

- Tell the children: if you get lost when out exploring, send a signal to let the others know where you are.
- Sit in a circle with a small group of children.
- Give the instruments to children sitting opposite each other across the circle.
- Tell the children that you can send secret signals to each other using the instruments.
- Demonstrate by using one of the instruments to play a simple rhythm.
- Ask the child with the same instrument to copy that rhythm.
- Encourage the children to take it in turns to play and copy rhythms.

Tip

The children would enjoy playing this game outside.

Activity 5

Aims and objectives

- Talking about instrumental sounds.
- Learning to use sound in imaginative ways.

Preparation

- Select pairs of instruments, e.g. two shakers, two drums, two bells, two tambourines

What to do

- After playing Activity 4 as a group, suggest that they have 'conversations' using the instruments.
- Allow one child to play a rhythm of their own choice, then, their partner plays an answer – a rhythm of his own choice or a repeat of the first rhythm as if talking to one another.
- Everyone listens to two children playing a conversation.
- Can they say if the conversation sounded happy or sad?
- Do they think someone is lost, worried, frightened or lonely?
- Maybe the children can try playing with some of these emotions in mind.

Activity 6

Aims and objectives

- Tuning into rhythm and rhyme.
- Learning to recognise that some words rhyme.

Preparation

- Have a pair of toy binoculars for this game (or simply use your hands to create some).

What to do

- Tell the children you are going on a bear hunt and you're going to spot things.
- But explain that everything that you see must rhyme with bear, e.g.

  'I am on a bear hunt – can I spy a chair?'

- Encourage the children to answer 'Yes'.

  'I am on a bear hunt can I spy a frog?'

- This time the children should answer 'No'.
- It will help the children if you repeat 'bear/chair' – or whatever word you are using. Does it rhyme?
- Other useful rhyming words include:

  fair
  stair
  pear
  Claire
  hare
  lair
  flare
  tear.

Tip

You may need to spend time with the children collecting some words that rhyme with bear before playing this game.

Activity 7

Aims and objectives

- Listening and remembering alliteration.
- Learning to hear the difference in sounds at the beginning of words.

Preparation

- Have a pair of toy binoculars for this game (or simply use your hands to create some).

What to do

- Tell the children you are going on a bear hunt and you're going to spot things, but explain that everything that you see must begin with the same sound as bear:

  'I am going on a bear hunt. Can I spy a . . .'

- The children must agree or disagree based on whether or not the word begins with /b/, e.g.

    ball
    bell
    bird
    baby
    bed
    bath
    bottle
    book
    bucket
    butterfly.

Whatever Next! by Jill Murphy

Another intrepid explorer sets out to visit strange and wonderful places.

Resources

- *Whatever Next!* by Jill Murphy (Activities 1, 2 & 3)
- Large and small bear (Activity 3)
- Percussion instruments and three different-sized bears (Activity 4)
- Tape recorder (Activity 5)
- A can of drink, a jar of honey, an apple and a packet of biscuits (Activity 7)
- Soft toys (bears and owl) and a blanket (Activity 7)

Tip

A great book to use when making junk model rockets or during a theme about bears.

Activity 1

Aims and objectives

- Listening and remembering voice sounds.
- Learning to listen for a target word and respond with associated sound.

Preparation

- Read the story to the children.

What to do

- After reading the words WHOOSH and BUMP – make appropriate sound effects, e.g. for BUMP – stamp your heel on the floor.
- At the end of the story ask if anyone noticed any special noises, and talk about them.

- Tell the children that you want them to make the sounds this time, but only when they hear the words WHOOSH or BUMP.
- Retell the two sentences again and enjoy the sound effects!
- There are other places in the story when these sounds could also be heard.
- Can the children suggest when? For example when the rocket lands on the moon.

Tip

Once the children are familiar with the story you can encourage them to retell it, remembering the order of the events.

Activity 2

Aims and objectives

- Talking about voice sounds.
- Learning to talk about different voice and speech sounds they make and hear.

Preparation

- You will need two bears – a large one and a small one.

What to do

- Read the story to the children.
- Show the children two bears. Ask which one could be Mrs Bear and which Baby Bear.
- Using an appropriate voice repeat a phrase from the story spoken by Mrs Bear, e.g.

  'Look at the state of you! Why, you look as if you've been up a chimney!'

- Ask which bear said that.

- Remind the children of Baby Bear's response.
- Invite one of the children to answer for Baby Bear with an appropriate voice.
- Let the children take turns, in pairs, to talk to each other as Mrs Bear and Baby.

Tip

Introduce a toy owl to encourage children to find a voice for the owl.

Activity 3

Aims and objectives

- Talking about instrumental sounds.
- Learning to use sound in imaginative ways.

Preparation

- You will need three bears of different sizes and a small selection of percussion instruments, for louder sounds and quieter ones.
- Read the story to the children.

What to do

- Ask the children:
  How many bears are in the story?
  Why is Baby Bear called Baby Bear?
  How tall do you think he is?
  How old do you think he is?
  Which of the three toy bears is Baby Bear?
  Which bear is smaller than Baby Bear?
  Have they remembered Teddy???
- Now decide which bear is which.
- Let the children choose an instrument to represent each bear.
- Take it in turns to play the instruments and move the appropriate bear.

Activity 4

Aims and objectives

- Listening and remembering environmental sounds.
- Learning to imitate sounds.

Preparation

- Read the story to the children.
- You will need a tape recorder.

What to do

- Tell the children you are going to make the sounds effects for the story.
- Use the pictures in the book to remind the children of the story.
- Ask for suggestions for the sound effects needed, e.g.
    Curtains opening and closing – rubbing hands together
    Finding the box – heaving sounds
    Owl flying – tapping cheeks with open mouth
    The aeroplane – roaring sound
    Landing on the moon – stamp foot
    Eating picnic – eating sounds
- Read the story with the sound effects onto tape.
- When they listen to the tape, encourage the children to talk about how they made the sounds.

Tip

It is useful to have two adults when making the recording, one to read the story and one to lead the sound effects.

Activity 5

Aims and objectives

- Talking about environmental sounds.
- Learning to place sounds in their context.

Preparation

- Read the story to the children.
- You will need a tape recorder.

What to do

- Working with a small group of children, talk about the sound effects needed and ask the children where we can hear those sounds in this building.
- Use a portable tape recorder to record children producing the actual sounds, e.g. opening curtains or dragging a box or running a tap.
- Play the tape to another group of children.
- Can they recognise the sounds?
- Play the sound effects in the appropriate places as the children retell the story.

Tip

Talk about what time of the day the story happens and how we know. Encourage the children to talk about bedtime routines like closing the curtains and having a bath.

Activity 6

Aims and objectives

- To speak confidently to adults and other children.
- Learning to talk about problems.

Preparation

- Provide a can of drink, a jar of honey, an apple and a packet of biscuits, soft toys and a blanket.
- Read the story to the children.

What to do

- Use the illustrations to work out what food Baby Bear took with him.
- Have these ready to give to the children.
- Look carefully at the picture of the picnic on the moon.
- What else did Baby Bear take?
- Can the children find some of these items in the room, e.g. a spoon.

- Count how many share the picnic.
- Arrange soft toys on a small blanket to represent Baby Bear, Teddy and Owl.
- Let the children share out the food between the three toys.
- How many biscuits each?

- Now suppose there was only Baby Bear and Teddy.
- What would happen when they shared out the biscuits?
- Try it and see.

- What about the apple, how will that be shared?
- Encourage the children to think of solutions.

- What about the honey?
- How many spoonfuls of honey are in the jar?
- How could we find out?
- How many spoonfuls could each toy have?

Tip

Talk about what Baby Bear is wearing as a helmet. Do the children know how a colander is used?

Variations

- What if Baby Bear had met some aliens on the moon?
- How many would have shared the picnic then?
- Encourage the children to make up new problems with more characters sharing the picnic.

Activity 7

Aims and objectives

- Listening and remembering voice sounds.
- Learning to listen for a target word and respond with associated sound.

Preparation

- Read the story to the children.
- You will need a large space for this activity.

What to do

- Sit in a circle.
- Tell the children to crouch down and pretend to be in their rocket.
- Count down from 5 and encourage them to join in with shouting 'Blast off!'
- The children pretend to blast off to the moon in their rockets and run around an open space.
- Clap your hands as a signal for everyone to stop and listen.
- Call out a number, e.g. 3.
- The children have to get into groups of three, then sit down together and pretend to eat their picnic.
- To repeat the game, call everyone back to form a circle.
- This time call out number 2 or 4.

Tip

This would be a good game to play outdoors on a fine day.

Tricky times

Sometimes things go wrong – even for explorers.

Tip

An opportunity to tackle problem solving using your everyday play resources.

Resources

- Selection of farm and zoo animals (Activity 1)
- Train track, farm animals, buildings and cars (Activity 4)
- Teddy bear and coloured paper or card and sticky shapes (Activity 5)
- Teddy bear and other soft toys (Activity 6)
- Plastic, play dough or pictures of food (Activity 6)

Activity 1

Aims and objectives

- Listening and remembering environmental sounds.
- Learning to identify sounds.

Preparation

- Put a mixture of animals from your farm and zoo sets into a bag.

What to do

- Some explorer has left the gates open! All the animals have got out.
- Can the children help Farmer Frank and Keeper Kelly to get them safely back again?
- The children take it in turns to dip into the bag and hold one of the animals in their hand, without letting anyone else see what it is.
- They make the sound of that animal.

- Can the others guess what it is?

- Everyone takes an animal and dances round the room. Children swap their animal with their friends as they do so.
- When the music stops the children have to find all the others who have the same animal by making the sounds and listening out for the sounds, all at the same time.

- The farmer and the zookeeper stand near the respective layouts or playmats.
- Everyone else has an animal chosen from the bag.
- In turn the farmer and the zookeeper make the noise of one of their animals. The child holding that animal takes it back to the farm or zoo. If you have more than one of each animal in the bag the sound can be repeated for another child to recognise.

Tip

Choose the animals carefully so that the children will know the sound – no camels or hippos!

Activity 2

Aims and objectives

- Listening and remembering sounds we can make.
- Learning to distinguish between sounds.

What to do

- Tell a story with actions and sound effects.
- The vehicle that the explorers are travelling in has broken down. What can be done to rescue them? e.g.

The explorers are driving their jeep along a dusty road.

The jeep won't stay in a straight line.

The explorer stops and gets out of the jeep to find out what is wrong.

The tyre has a puncture and the air is leaking out.

Get out your phone and call for help

. . . and so on.

- Encourage the children to solve the problem in other ways.
- Continue the story . . .
- The explorers are in their jeep. When they arrive at their destination – the jungle, the wild wood – they can't open the door. How can they get out? Send for the police? Send for the mechanic?
- What sounds would they hear? Make some sounds and let the children guess who is coming to help them.
- Make the sound of, e.g. a drill, metal being prised open, a hammer. What's the mechanic using to get the door open?
- How will the story end?

Activity 3

Aims and objectives

- Listening and remembering sounds we can make.
- Learning to distinguish between sounds.

Preparation

- You will need a large space for this activity.

What to do

- The children 'drive' round in 'cars' making appropriate noises – but not too loud or they might miss the signal.
- The adult gives the signal to stop.

Either

- Either the adult makes a 'phhhhhh' noise representing the air leaving a punctured tyre, and the children stop, kneel down and look at their 'tyre'. Then the adult makes the wailing sound of a siren as rescue arrives and the children wave to show where they are.

Or

- Or the adult calls out 'emergency' and the children make their siren noises, and then the adult beeps the horn to let the children know that they should switch the sirens off as everything is sorted.
- Then off they go again.

Tip

Try clapping your hands or raising an arm above your head as the signal to listen.

Activity 4

Aims and objectives

- Listening and remembering sounds we can make.
- Learning to remember patterns of sounds.

Preparation

- You will need a train track set out and farm animals, buildings, cars, etc. to add interest to the layout.

What to do

- Tell the children Terry the train driver has lost his map. He's not sure where he should be driving the train to today. Can you help everyone to get to their destination?
- Place the train at the station on your train track. Help the children to work out the identity of the places he will pass through, e.g. a field with cows or a building with a clock.
- For each place or feature around the track, work out a suitable sound effect.
- Children take it in turns to be Terry and guide the train round the track with everyone else making the sound effects of the journey.
- The children can try to remember the pattern of the sounds when there is a different starting and finishing point, e.g. Mrs Green gets on near the field of cows and gets off at the next town.

- What sounds will she hear? Children should make the noises in the order she will pass them on her journey.

- Repeat this with other figures going on other journeys around this same track.

- The adult makes the sounds for three consecutive features around the track. Who can tell you where that train starts and finishes? The children can move the train to demonstrate or check their answer.

Activity 5

Aims and objectives

- Talking about rhythm and rhyme.
- Learning to make up a series of rhyming words.

Preparation

- You will need coloured paper or card and sticky shapes for decoration.

What to do

- Tell the children, 'It's Teddy's birthday and we haven't got anything ready for his party. Can anybody help?'
- Make some hats and some placemats ready for the party. Talk about the shapes (cones or cylinders for hats, rectangles or squares for the mats) and use sticky paper shapes to decorate them.
- Tell the children both of these words (hat and mat) rhyme.
- Make up some silly sentences together using some rhyming words while the children work on their hats and mats, e.g.

  The rat ate the mat
  The fat cat wore a hat
  The bat sat on the mat
  The gnat bit the rat
  The rat and the cat had a chat.

- Remind the children the party is for Teddy (or any other doll or toy).
- Can the children find names that rhyme with Teddy? E.g.
    Eddie
    Neddy
    Freddie.
- Make some funny names up keeping the rhyme going.

Tip

These activities will work equally well with the dolls in the home play area or on a smaller scale in the doll's house.

Activity 6

Aims and objectives

- Talking about alliteration.
- Learning to select a range of words that start with the same sound.

Preparation

- You will need a teddy and some other dolls or soft toys.
- Decide on the dolls' names that start with the same sound as some food.
- Provide toy food, plastic or play dough, or pictures of the food.

What to do

- Name the dolls and show the children the food ready for the party.
- Tell the children that guests can only eat food that starts with the same sound as their own name.
- Can the children work out who can eat which food? E.g.
    Henry: ham sandwiches, honey cakes
    Travis: tuna sandwiches, treacle tart
    Carl: crisps, cookies
    Sam: sausages, strawberries
    Pushba: pizza, pears.
- Let the children put the food or pictures next to the toys.

- Now talk about who else is coming to the party.
- Teddy said only people with names that start with the same sound as Teddy could come.
- Think of as many names as you can with the children, e.g.
    Thomas
    Tim
    Tracy
    Tilly
    Ted
    Toby
    Tina
    Tilak.
- Give all the children one of these names and they can all come to the party!

Counting rhymes

Take the chance to include some phonic games as well as practising counting.

Resources

- A fishing game with cardboard fish and paper clips (Activity 2)
- Two buckets (Activity 2 – variation)

Tip

These activities will adapt to fit many different counting rhymes.

Activity 1

Aims and objectives

- Listening and remembering environmental sounds.
- Learning to imitate sounds.

Preparation

- Learn the rhyme – 'Five little speckled frogs'.
- A good activity for outdoors.

What to do

- This is a great rhyme for sound effects!
- Frogs can croak as well as saying 'yum-yum' in this rhyme.
- What about the bugs that the frogs are eating?
- Practise the individual sounds first and then add them in to the rhyme as you say it.
- Play this outdoors:
    Fifteen 'bugs' crawl around or run around 'flying' while humming or buzzing.

> Five frogs chase them and catch one each.
> Sing the first verse.
> - The remaining ten bugs are then chased by the remaining four frogs.
>   Again they catch one each and then all sing the second verse
> - And so on until all the bugs are eaten and all the frogs are in
>   the pond.

Tip

A less active alternative would be to make 'bugs' from recycled materials, and get children to dangle them on strings for the frogs to 'catch' before you sing.

Activity 2

Aims and objectives

- Tuning into alliteration.
- Learning to identify the initial sounds in words.

Preparation

- Learn the rhyme – '1, 2, 3, 4, 5, once I caught a fish alive'.
- Use a traditional 'fishing' game – each cardboard fish needs to have a picture on it.

What to do

- Make a simple fishing game with the children. Each cardboard fish needs to have a picture on it, and a paper clip. Tie magnets to fishing rods and catch your fish by attracting the paper clip.
- Say the rhyme through as each child in turn fishes.
- When he has caught a fish he says the name of the object pictured on it, and then says its initial sound, e.g.
  - cat /k/
  - table /t/
  - granny /g/
  - shoes /sh/.
- Then the next child has a go at fishing, as you all sing again.

Tip

Match the pictures to your current theme – animals, household objects, transport, holidays, etc.

Variation

- Limit the objects pictured on the fish to just two initial sounds.
- Have two buckets in different colours or designs.
- When the child has caught a fish, identified the picture and its initial sound, the fish is placed in the correct bucket, e.g. all the /k/ sounds in one bucket and all the /p/ sounds in the other.

Activity 3

Aims and objectives

- To extend vocabulary.
- Learning to use positional language.

Preparation

- Learn the rhyme – 'Five little ducks went swimming one day'.

What to do

- Say the rhyme and perform the actions with the children.
- Draw their attention to the words 'over the hills' and its action.
- Ask the children: where else might the little ducks go? Collect their ideas.
- Modify the rhyme with some of these ideas.
- The children will need to choose:
  - a word to describe the position – over, across, under, etc.
  - a word to describe a feature or place – house, bridge, etc.
- To use these in the rhyme and keep the rhythm correct you will need a positional word of two syllables and a place word of one syllable, e.g.
    across the road
    *   *   *

    behind the tree
    *   *   *

under the bridge

*   *   *

near the shop

*   *   *

around the hedge

*   *   *

- Sing and mime to the new words.

Activity 4

Aims and objectives

- Tuning into sounds we can make.
- Learning to keep in time.

Preparation

- Learn the rhyme – 'Five little firemen'.

What to do

- Say the rhyme and the actions that go with it.
- On the second line: '1, 2, 3, 4, 5 they go' – the children point to one finger for each number they say.
- The second time you sing it: they point to their fingers and say '1, 2, 3, 4, hmmm'.
- The third time: – '1, 2, 3, hmmm, hmmm'.
- And so on until you reach five hmmms!
- Children should still be pointing and keeping the beat correct.

Tip

Dress five children up in yellow helmets and wellies to look like firemen. Let them march in time to the beat as you say this rhyme.

Activity 5

Aims and objectives

- Listening and remembering sounds we can make.
- Learning to distinguish between sounds.

Preparation

- Learn the rhyme – 'Two little dicky birds'.
- A good outdoor activity.

What to do

- Once the children are familiar with the rhyme try playing this game outdoors.
- One child is kept indoors until the others have hidden a toy bird somewhere in the grounds.
- The child then comes out to look for it.
- The other children give clues by repeating a 'tweeting' sound, getting louder and louder as he nears the bird, but quieter if he moves away.

Variation

- A more difficult version would be to hide two birds and have two groups of children hunting at the same time.
- Choose two contrasting bird sounds, and split the children into two groups, one for each bird. You could try 'tweet, tweet' and 'tu-whit-tu-woo'.

Part 4
Knowledge and understanding of the world

Chapter 7
Starting with a walk

Finding out about their local environment is an important element of children's growing knowledge and understanding of the world. Going out for a walk is a popular way to introduce the children to the place they live in. By concentrating on the sounds they can hear around them children will be developing their listening skills and their phonic awareness.

What might we hear?

Choose an activity to prepare the children for the walk.

Resources

- Clip art of outdoor environmental sounds (Activities 1 & 2)
- Two copies of a simple map of your walk (Activity 2)

Tip

Preparing children in this way helps them to tune into the activity.

Activity 1

Aims and objectives

- Tuning into environmental sounds.
- Learning to be aware of sounds around them.

Preparation

- Using pictures available on your computer, print out multiple copies of pictures of things that you might hear on a particular walk. Include some 'red herrings'.

What to do

- Each child chooses five pictures of things that he thinks he will hear on this walk, and sticks them onto a piece of paper.
- On returning, the children can circle each of the sounds if and when they heard it on the walk.
- They can then add any other sounds that they heard, but hadn't included in the chosen five.

Tip

Instead of computer-generated pictures you could draw some simple outline pictures for the children to choose from. On return the ones that were heard could be coloured in.

Activity 2

Aims and objectives

- Tuning into environmental sounds.
- Learning to recall sounds.

Preparation

- Prepare lots of small pictures, hand-drawn or computer-generated, of things you might hear on your walk.
- Provide two copies of a simple 'map' or pictorial route of your walk (one small and one large enough to use with the group of children).

What to do

- Ask the children what they think they will hear.
- Stick pictures on the large map where the children think these sounds will be heard, e.g. they might want to stick a picture of a car on the main road, or a bird near the trees.
- Take the small copy of the route with you and record your findings on it as you go – quick drawings with labels.
- Compare this with the large 'map' on your return.
  - Were the sounds where you thought they would be?
  - Did you hear anything that surprised you?
  - Did you hear all of the sounds that you expected to hear?

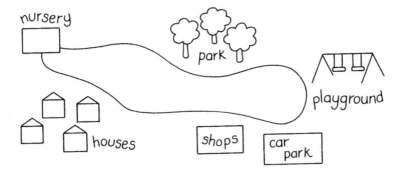

Activity 3

Aims and objectives

- Talking about environmental sounds.
- Learning to place sounds in their context.

What to do

- Spend some time before you set off talking with the children about what they think they'll hear, and why.
- Discuss where you might hear any sound they suggest.
- Suggest ideas to the children, including some odd ideas, e.g.
  - Will we hear a trumpet in the park?
  - Will we hear children at the play area?
  - Will we hear a cat in the street?
  - Will we hear a lion in the car park?
- Allow time for the children to explain their responses as they think through potential sounds. Some children might be quite imaginative in their ideas and they need time and encouragement to think 'outside the box'!
- Introduce concepts such as 'probably', 'possibly', 'unlikely', 'sometimes', 'maybe', 'never', 'occasionally', 'now and then' according to your children's abilities.

What did we hear?

Make time to talk about your walk as soon as possible after you get back.

Resources

- Digital camera or notepad and pen (Activity 1)
- *The Listening Walk* by Paul Showers (Activity 1)
- Tape recorder (Activity 2)

Activity 1

Aims and objectives

- Tuning into environmental sounds.
- Learning to recall sounds.

Preparation

- On the walk take digital photos, or make a list of drawings, words or symbols for the sounds that you hear in the order you hear them.

What to do

- On your return from the walk discuss the sounds that you heard.
  - What did we hear?
  - Where did we hear it?
  - Did we hear the same sound in more than one place?
  - Were you surprised by any of the sounds that you heard? Why?
- Can the children list the sounds in the order they heard them?
- Use the photos or drawings as prompts to help you and the children.
- Read the book *The Listening Walk* by Paul Showers.
- Compare this walk with the one you have been on.

Tip

If you have been on several walks recently compare the findings of one walk with another. 'Today we heard a . . . at . . . Are we likely to hear that sound again if we go to . . .?'

Activity 2

Aims and objectives

- Listening and remembering environmental sounds.
- Learning to identify sounds.

Preparation

- Take a portable tape recorder with you and record some of the sounds as you walk.

Tip

The children would have to be completely silent if you wanted to record something like birdsong, but will enjoy contributing to other noises like chatter, footsteps walking or running and laughter.

What to do

- When you get back, play the tape.
- Can the children identify the sounds?
- Can other children not included on the walk recognise any of the sounds?
- How many sounds can you hear?
    birds
    cars
    lorries
    buses
    wind in the trees
    footsteps on different kinds of surfaces
    voices, and whose is it?
    horn
    roadworks
    click of a gate, etc.

Paint a picture

Use the children's art work to inspire some speaking and listening activities.

Resources

- Paints, brushes and paper (Activity 1)
- Taped music and drum (Activity 2)
- Paper, paints, glue and objects collected on the walk (Activity 3)

Tip

If your children are not yet able to create a recognisable image, encourage them to use a colour or different marks to represent the sounds heard. An adult can write underneath what sound each abstract symbol represents.

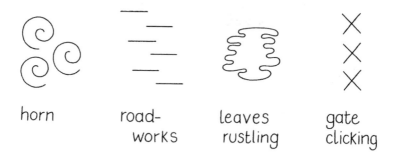

horn   road-works   leaves rustling   gate clicking

Activity 1

Aims and objectives

- Tuning into environmental sounds.
- Learning to describe sounds.

Preparation

- A selection of paper and paint should be available so that on returning from your walk the children can each paint one of the things that made a sound that you heard.

- Cut out and mount each picture. (You may need repeats of pictures, so don't worry if some of the children want to paint the same thing.)

What to do

- Arrange the pictures along a wall, or peg them onto a 'washing line'.
- Can the children do this in the order in which you heard them?

- Choose a child to point to the pictures slowly and in order.
- As he points the others make an appropriate noise/sound effect to recreate the sounds you heard on your walk.

- Point to the pictures in a random fashion.
- Children make sound effects as before, but will have to be watching carefully not just anticipating what comes next.

Tip

If you recorded the sounds as you went along – either as a quick sketch for the children to refer to, or a list for yourself – this will help you all at this point.

Activity 2

Aims and objectives

- Tuning into environmental sounds.
- Learning to discriminate between sounds.

Preparation

- Choose three or four of the paintings made after the walk (See Activity 1) and place them in different corners of the room.

What to do

- Remind the children of what sounds these pictures represent.
- Agree with them an appropriate sound or noise for each one.
- Have a practice!

- An adult can play some music or beat a drum while the children dance in the middle of the room.
- The adult stops playing; the children stop and listen, as an adult, or a chosen child, makes one of the noises.
- The children have to go to the corner where that picture is displayed.

Activity 3

Aims and objectives

- Tuning into environmental sounds.
- Learning to recall sounds.

Preparation

- Use any small items that the children collected on their walk.
- Paper, glue and paint.

What to do

- The children draw or paint individual pictures or create their own collages of 'our walk'.
- They can stick onto it any of the small items they collected on the walk that remind them of sounds that they heard, e.g. a leaf, a feather, a small stone.
- This is an opportunity for the children to express themselves freely.
- How do individual children represent the sounds that they heard?
- Is the walk shown as a route or a map?
- Can any of the children tell you about the sounds that are in their pictures?

Creating music

Have fun with singing and music making after your walk.

Resources

- A selection of instruments: home-made and commercially produced (Activities 1, 2 & 3)
- Children's own pictures of things that make sounds (Activity 2)
- Multiple copies of pictures of things heard on your walk (Activity 3)
- Everyday items that make a noise (Activity 4)
- Metal or wooden beaters in pots (Activity 4)

Activity 1

Aims and objectives

- Talking about instrumental sounds.
- Learning to match sounds to instruments.

Preparation

- Set up a sound table, providing objects or percussion instruments that might make a good representation of the sounds that you heard on your walk, e.g.
    coconut shells
    clackers
    castanets
    wood blocks
    pan lid and wooden spoon
    shakers
    drums
    triangles
    bells
    chime bars
    horn
    squeaky toys
    card
    tissue paper

yoghurt pots
strings of beads.

Tip

Include household items and home-made instruments as well as commercially produced percussion instruments in your selection.

What to do

- Encourage the children to investigate and experiment with the instruments over the session, to create sounds heard on the walk.
- Come together so that the children can share their choices with the group.
- Let the children explain their choices.
- Discuss together whether they have chosen an appropriate instrument, e.g. George wants to use the biggest drum to represent the sound of a bird!
- Is this a good idea?

Activity 2

Aims and objectives

- Tuning into sounds we can make.
- Learning to keep in time.

Preparation

- Use the pictures created by the children in 'Paint a picture', Activity 1, see page 186.
- Use the instruments from the sound table you have set up.

What to do

- Remind the children of what the pictures are. What sound did they make?
- Each child chooses one of the sound-making objects from the music table and uses their instrument to work out a sound effect for one of the pictures.
- Make sure that you have one sound per picture.
- Position the children so that every child can see the pictures clearly.
- All together, play a slow, steady beat with your hands – clapping, slapping thighs, etc.
- Count in fours as you do this, keeping a regular beat. 1-2-3-4, 1-2-3-4 . . .
- Once the rhythm is going well introduce the sounds for the pictures:
  1-2-3 on '4' the child with the sound maker for the first picture makes the noise.
  Count to 4 again, and on '4' the second sound is made and so on along the line of pictures.
- Once the children are able to do this, keeping the beat going, point randomly at the pictures to keep the children watching and listening attentively.

Activity 3

Aims and objectives

- Tuning into sounds we can make.
- Learning to make up patterns of sounds.

Preparation

- You will need multiple copies of pictures of three things that you heard on your walk.
- For each picture have an instrument that will make a suitable sound effect.
- Place three pictures – one of each – where the children can see them.

What to do

- Remind the children of what the pictures show.
- Let the children test the instruments and agree on which one will be used to represent each sound picture.
- Point to each picture in turn, and the children will play the matching instrument.
    bird, bus, people chattering.
- Rearrange the three pictures and play again.
    bird, people chattering, bus.
- Keep doing this until everyone has had a turn to play.
- Use additional copies of the picture to make a repeating pattern of sound, e.g. bird, bus, people chattering, bird, bus, people chattering, bird, bus, people chattering,
- How many different ways can we arrange these three sounds? E.g.
    bus, horn, people chattering,
    horn, bus, people chattering
    people chattering, bus, horn.

Tip

Leave the pictures and the instruments out for the children to make up their own repeating patterns

Activity 4

Aims and objectives

- Talking about environmental sounds.
- Learning to talk about sounds they can create.

Preparation

- Set up a sound walk in your setting, indoors and outdoors.
- Adults can prepare this for the children to discover, or involve the children in its creation.
- To do this, choose objects that make sounds and provide pots containing wooden or metal beaters near each site.

- Try:

  metal objects: pans, pan lids, spoons, colanders

  plastic bottles securely sealed, with pebbles, rice, pasta, etc

  indoor wind chimes

  up-turned pots and buckets

  rows of posts or fence palings to run a wooden beater along.

What to do

- Allow plenty of time for the children to explore the sound walk in their own way.

- Work with a small group to make up words that represent the sounds you can make.
- Ask the children if they have a favourite sound.
- Can they describe it?
    - Why do you like it?
    - Is it quiet, loud, tinkling, etc?

- An adult can record the various sounds that can be made on this walk.
- Be creative in how you make these sounds to set a challenge for the children.
- Play one of the sounds to the children. Can they identify it?
    - What makes that noise?
    - How was the sound created?
    - Test it out, and investigate if not sure.

- Play a sound and then ask the children if they can recreate it.

Talk the walk

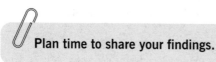

Plan time to share your findings.

Resources

- Small objects representing things you heard on your walk (Activity 6)
- A small bag or box (Activity 6)
- Cardboard boxes and sugar paper (Activity 8)

Activity 1

Aims and objectives

- Talking about instrumental sounds.
- Learning to express an opinion about different sounds.

What to do

- After you have been for a walk make time to talk with the children about the sounds that they heard.
- Ask questions to encourage discussion of personal preferences:
  - Which of the sounds did you like?
  - Which of the sounds did you not like?
  - Why?
  - Do we all agree?
- Make a pictogram of 'our favourite sounds' choosing from those that were heard on the walk.

Tip

These open-ended questions encourage personal choice. There is no right or wrong answer here, and children's preferences will vary. Accepting this fact is a positive step in the children's social development.

Activity 2

Aims and objectives

- Tuning into environmental sounds.
- Learning to discriminate between sounds.

What to do

- If you have been on more than one walk recently engage the children in a discussion to compare sounds from different walks, e.g.
  the park
  a shopping street
  a residential street
  the nursery grounds
  a busy road.
- Did we hear any sounds in more than one place?
- What were they?
- Were there more sounds in one place than in another?
- Which was the noisiest walk?
- Are some places quieter (or louder) than others?
- Can you put the sounds into sets? E.g.
  - **quiet/loud**
    bird/train
    rain/workmen
  - **natural/man-made**
    trees/cars
    wind/pelican crossing.

Activity 3

Aims and objectives

- Tuning into environmental sounds.
- Learning to recall sounds.

What to do

- Sit in a circle to play a simple memory game, each child in turn adding to the list of things that were heard.
  Child One: 'When we went to the park we heard leaves rustling.'
  Child Two: 'When we went to the park we heard leaves rustling and birds singing.'
  Child Three: 'When we went to the park we heard leaves rustling, birds singing and children shouting.'
  etc.
- **Try it this way for younger children**:
- Everyone says 'When we went to the park we heard . . .'
- Then Child One stands up, says and acts out his choice . . . 'a bird' And then sits down again.
- Everyone says 'When we went to the park we heard . . .'
- Child One stands up, says and acts out his choice again, and then Child Two stands up, says and acts out his choice and then they both sit down.
- Continue round the group, with a new choice added to the originals each time.

Activity 4

Aims and objectives

- Tuning into rhythm and rhyme.
- Learning to experience and enjoy rhythm and rhyme.

What to do

- The children can say and act out:
  'We are going down the street
  Listen to our walking *feet*
  Walk, walk, walk, walk.'
- Encourage the children to keep to the rhythm as they speak and move.

- Change the action words each time, e.g.
    stamping
    jumping
    hopping
    marching
    striding
    dancing.

Tip

This is a good activity for outdoors – or any other large space.

Activity 5

Aims and objectives

- Talking about rhythm and rhyme.
- Learning to complete sentences using rhyming words.

What to do

- Remind the children about the term 'rhyme'. Give them some examples of pairs of words that rhyme.
- Explain that you are all going to make up some simple rhymes.
- Say a sentence that rhymes, e.g.

    The big brown dog/sat next to the old green frog.

- Then repeat it, pausing before the last word – the one that rhymes.
    - Can the children give the rhyme?
    - Can they think of an alternative rhyme?
- You could say the initial sound of the last word to help children along.
- Now try some more sentences, e.g.

    'In the park we heard a /l/' . . . 'lark'
    'In the street we heard our /f/' . . . 'feet'
    'We heard people talk when we went on our /w/' . . . 'walk'
    'We'll hear a duck with a bit of /l/' . . . 'luck'
    'The sound of a bird is what we /h/' . . . 'heard'
    'There were noisy feet going down the /s/' . . . 'street'.

Tip

Be careful about your choice of words!

Activity 6

Aims and objectives

- Listening and remembering sounds we can make.
- Learning to identify sounds and their sources.

Preparation

- You will need some small objects representing sounds that you heard on your walk and a small bag or box to put them in.

What to do

- Place the objects in the bag.
- Show them to the children as you put them in and discuss the sounds they made, e.g.

   a car, a bus, a bird, a doll/figure, a sheep.

- One child reaches in and holds an object of their choice (out of sight of the others).
- They make the noise, and the others guess what has been chosen.
- They then show the object before replacing it in the bag.
- Let each child have a turn at choosing.

Activity 7

Aims and objectives

- Tuning into oral blending and segmenting.
- Learning to blend phonemes into words.

Tip

Remember to use the sounds not the spelling when you segment words.

What to do

- Start by having an adult segment the words.
- Avoid complex words and words that start with two separate consonant sounds (words such as 'tractor' or 'plane').
- Say, e.g. 'When we walked down the street we heard a b-ir-d'.
- Encourage the children to blend the sounds back into a word to find out what you are thinking of.
- You could also try these words:
  c-ar
  d-i-gg-er
  h-or-n
  m-a-n
  b-e-ll.
- A child could then have a go at segmenting a word into phonemes. You may have to whisper a suitable word to them – keep to three sounds at first, e.g. bus, bike, bell, cat, dog, leaf.

Activity 8

Aims and objectives

- Listening and remembering environmental sounds.
- Learning to imitate sounds.

Preparation

- You will need a selection of large cardboard boxes and some sugar paper.
- The exact requirements will depend on where you went for your walk.

What to do

- With the children, make a simple representation of your route. Try using:
  - boxes for buildings
  - coloured paper for other features: green for the park, blue for a river, etc.

- When it's complete, ask the children to work out where the various sounds they heard came from, e.g.

  We heard birds as we went past the park.

- One or two children can then stand at that spot on your 'walk' and make the appropriate sound effect.
- Position the children for all of the sounds that you have included.
- When everyone is in position and quiet, one child or adult can walk along the route you took. As they pass each 'sound' that child makes the sound.
- Let another person do the walk or all change places and be another sound.

Variation

- If you can set this up in a large space – or outdoors – children could vary the volume of their sound effect: starting quietly, getting louder as the walker comes towards them, then getting quieter, and back to very quiet as the walker moves on past them. By then, the next sound is starting to be heard. This encourages great cooperation between the children.

Whatever the weather

Take advantage of weather variations.

Resources

- A rainy day (Activity 1)
- Plastic sheeting, parachute, umbrellas, buckets (Activity 1)
- Sand and water tray with sound-making equipment (Activity 1)
- A snowy day (Activity 2)
- Old wellingtons, paint and large sheets of paper (Activity 2)
- A foggy day (Activity 3)
- One or two percussion instruments and some cloths (Activity 3)
- Visiting musician (optional) (Activities 3 & 4)
- A windy day (Activity 4)
- Pen and paper, percussion instruments, wind chimes and a recorder
  (Activity 4).

Tip

Don't restrict your walks to fine, dry and warm days. As long as the children are dressed appropriately they can enjoy walks in most weather conditions – but don't go too far in case the weather gets worse or someone falls over.

Activity 1

Aims and objectives

- Listening and remembering environmental sounds.
- Learning to imitate sounds.

Preparation

- Dress the children for rainy weather.
- Outside you will need – umbrellas, parachute and plastic sheeting, buckets and containers.
- Back indoors you will need – sand and water tray with sound-making equipment.

What to do

- Take the children outside and listen for the different sound effects the rain can make:

    go inside the shed and listen to the rain on the shed roof

    stretch out some plastic sheeting on the ground

    use a parachute to stand underneath

    carry umbrellas

    have a bucket or other containers in different materials – plastic, metal – and listen to the rain splashing into them, or onto the water they contain.

- Encourage the children wearing wellingtons to splash in puddles.
- What sounds can you make?
- Collect words – real and made up, e.g. splash. splodge, shlurp.
- When you are back indoors ask the children to recreate some of these sounds.
- Try:
    - sand sieved onto crumpled paper, tissue paper or a metal baking tray
    - the water-wheel or a watering can in your water tray.

Activity 2

Aims and objectives

- Talking about environmental sounds.
- Learning to make up words to describe sounds.

Preparation

- Dress the children for snowy weather.
- Back indoors you will need – old wellingtons, paint and large sheets of paper.

What to do

- Once the snow has settled on the ground, wrap up, put on your wellies and head out.
- Look at your footprints in the snow.
- Make up words to represent the sounds that you make with your feet, e.g. scrunch, crunch.
- Can they be made into a snow-walking rhyme?
    'This is the way we scrunch our feet, scrunch our feet, scrunch
        our feet
    This is the way we scrunch our feet
    On a cold and snowy Monday.'
- **When you are back indoors,** talk about how you made footprints in the snow where you have walked.
- Dip old wellies in paint and 'walk' them down a long strip of paper to show the route of your walk.
- Can you make the sounds you created outside?

Tip

Keep an old pair of wellies available for making paint prints.

Activity 3

Aims and objectives

- Tuning into environmental sounds.
- Learning to discriminate between sounds.

Preparation

- Dress the children for foggy weather.
- Outside you will need – one or two percussion instruments.
- Back indoors you will need – percussion instruments and some cloths.
- A visiting musician (optional).

What to do

- Talk about the effects of fog before setting out.
- Discuss with the children how you can't see very well in the fog, you have to feel and listen. If you were out near a road this would be very important. Make sure they understand this message.
- Discuss how sounds are muffled in the fog and it's not so easy to hear.
- Take some percussion instruments when you go outside.
- Use the percussion instruments to make a noise at a distance.
- Encourage the children to talk about what it sounds like.
- **When you are back indoors** try to muffle some instruments to create different sounds, e.g. a drum can be covered with a cloth.
- Compare the sounds with and without the cloth.
- A local musician or some secondary-school children may be willing to come in and demonstrate using a muffle on a trumpet.

Activity 4

Aims and objectives

- Listening and remembering instrumental sounds.
- Learning to discriminate between loud and soft sounds.

Tip

For more ideas for a windy day see Playtime Activity 7, Chapter 9, p. 256.

Preparation

- Dress the children warmly.
- Back indoors you will need – pen and paper, wind chime, percussion instruments and a recorder and a visiting musician (optional).

What to do

- Talk about the noises that the wind makes.
- Make up words to represent the wind, from gentle breezes to a gale.
- Discuss quiet to loud sounds made by the wind.
- Draw some symbols that show the children – very quiet, quiet, normal, loud, very loud.
- Make a 'wind' sounds such as 'ooooooooo' and as you point to the volume symbol children vary their sound in response.

- Talk about the noises that the wind causes other things to make.
- Collect a variety of wind chimes ranging from high-pitched, tinkling to resonant bass sounds.
- Make up words to describe the different noises they make.
- Ask the children to find instruments that make similar noises.
- Can they make the connection that higher sounds come from smaller, thinner instruments and that lower sounds come from larger instruments?
- Show the children some instruments that you blow down.

- A local musician or a group of musicians from a local brass band may be willing to come in and demonstrate their skills, and let children hear the differences in the various instruments.
- Ask the musicians to demonstrate that higher sounds come from smaller, thinner instruments and that lower sounds come from larger instruments.

Tip

Don't forget – staff and parents may have hidden musical talent!

When shall we walk?

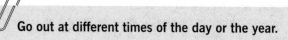

Go out at different times of the day or the year.

Resources

- Digital or video camera (Activity 2)
- Photographs from an earlier walk (Activity 2)

Tip

Focus on sounds for a short period during a more general walk or visit.

Activity 1

Aims and objectives

- Listening and remembering environmental sounds.
- Learning to develop vocabulary.

Preparation

- Plan to take the same short walk on two consecutive days – or even twice on the same day if the children can manage that.

What to do

- Use a route that is close to your setting, and go on the same walk at different times of day.
- Encourage the children to be aware of the noises that stay the same and of the noises that change, or are missing.
  - Can you hear different things in the morning?
  - Is it noisier at lunchtime?
- Talk about changes and why this might happen.
- Discuss preferences: 'I like it better when . . . '.
- Encourage children to respect each other's choices, even if they are different from their own.

Variations

- Take a walk by the shops at Christmas time. What special sounds can you hear? Carols, bells, etc.
- Visit the same street with and then without a market. Compare the sounds.

Activity 2

Aims and objectives

- Talking about environmental sounds.
- Learning to place sounds in their context.

Preparation

- Outside you will need – digital or video camera.
- Back indoors you will need – some photographs or a video from an earlier walk.

What to do

- Do the same walk in summer and winter.
- Compare your findings.
- You will need a record of the first walk to show the children, such as a video or set of photographs. This will all help them to remember what it was like.
- Before you go on your walk, look at the video or photographs from an earlier walk.
- Discuss with the children:
  - When did we go on that walk?
  - Is the weather the same today?
  - What is different?
  - What did we hear then?
  - Do you think we will hear the same things today as we did then?
- On your return from the second walk, discuss with the children:
  - What did we hear today?
  - Did we hear all the same things as the first time we went?
  - What was different today?
  - What was new today?
  - What was the same?
- Seasonal walks can be opportunities to notice the changes that occur, e.g. do you hear birds in all seasons?

Tip

What special sounds are there in autumn when you walk near trees?
Bring a bag full of dry leaves back with you – make up words to represent the sounds.

Activity 3

Aims and objectives

- Tuning into environmental sounds.
- Learning to be aware of sounds around them.

What to do

- Take a small group of children through your setting, including areas they wouldn't usually go, such as the office and the kitchen.
- Go at different times of the day and compare your findings.
  - Which areas are quieter?
  - Can you hear your footsteps in this room?
  - Is there a sound in here that you can't hear anywhere else in your school or nursery?
  - What machines did you hear?
  - Did you recognise anyone's voice?
- List the sounds that you hear in the different places.
- Compare these to the outdoor sounds you have heard.

Imaginary walks

Use stories and rhymes for inspiration.

Resources

- Selection of instruments and sound makers (Activity 1)
- Props from your role play area to suit your story (Activity 1)
- *Choo, Choo, Clickety Clack* by Margaret Mayo and Alex Ayliffe (Activity 2)
- *The Wheels on the Bus* illustrated by Annie Kubler (optional) (Activity 3)
- *Rosie's Walk by* Pat Hutchins (Activity 4)

Tip

Always read and enjoy the story first before doing any work based on it.

Activity 1

Aims and objectives

- Talking about environmental sounds.
- Learning to place sounds in their context.

Preparation

- Set up a listening walk connected with the theme of your role play.
- You will also need a selection of instruments and objects that make sounds.
- Chose some props from your role play area suitable to the theme for your walk.
- Walks to create could include:
  - Woods with birds, animals and leaves: *Little Red Riding Hood*; *Goldilocks and the Three Bears.*
  - Street with vehicles, people, dogs: our town; our street.
  - Collections of animals: the farm, the zoo; the jungle.
  - Seagulls, fog horn, waves: the seaside; pirates.

Tip

For more ideas see *Nursery Rhymes* and the fairy stories in *It's Showtime!*.

What to do

- Discuss the scene for your walk with the children:
    - What sounds would there be?
    - How can they create these sounds?
- Let the children make the sounds, using their voices or instruments or noisy objects.
    - Where will the sounds occur along this particular walk?
- Create the walk and the sound effects with the children.
- Children then take their friend, their mummy or their teddy on the walk encouraging them to listen for the sounds.

Activity 2

Aims and objectives

- Tuning into sounds we can make.
- Learning to recreate sounds with a variety of different rhythms, speeds and volume.

Tip

Try creating your own sound dances when you are doing work based on a building site, or machines and diggers.

Preparation

- You will need *Choo, Choo, Clickety Clack* by Margaret Mayo and Alex Ayliffe, or other titles in this series by Orchard Books.
- A drum or tambour is optional.

What to do

- Read *Choo, Choo, Clickety Clack*, by Margaret Mayo and Alex Ayliffe.
- Make movements to represent activities or machines.
- Add sound effects with voices, e.g. clicking, hissing, clunk, tick and bang!
    Or sounds we can make, e.g. clicking fingers, clapping hands, stamping feet, slapping thighs – just your own of course!
- An adult could provide a rhythmic beat on a drum or tambour as the children perform their dances.

Activity 3

Aims and objectives

- Tuning into sounds we can make.
- Learning to join in with words and actions in songs.

What to do

- Sing 'The wheels on the bus' using only sound effect verses, e.g.
    the horn on the bus goes beep, beep, beep
    the windscreen wipers go swish, swash, swish
    the brakes on the bus go screeeeeeeeech.
- Adapt 'The wheels on the bus' to fit your walk.
- Encourage the children to add their own verses, e.g.
    the dogs on the walk went 'woof'
    the cats on the walk went 'miaou'
    the horses on the walk went 'neigh'.

    the bees in the park go 'zzz'
    the birds in the park go 'tweet'
    the leaves in the park go 'rustle'.

    The cars on the road go 'brrrrm'
    The motorbikes on the road go 'eee-ow'
    The police cars on the road go 'ee-or, ee-or'.

Tip

Child's Play International Ltd publish a colourful, bold version of this rhyme, illustrated by Annie Kubler.

Activity 4

Aims and objectives

- Listening and remembering sounds we can make.
- Learning to create sounds for stories.

Preparation

- Enjoy reading *Rosie's Walk* by Pat Hutchins.

What to do

- With the children, make a model of Rosie's walk using boxes or tables and chairs to represent the various places she passes. Take ideas from the illustrations in the book.
- What might she hear as she walks around?
- Act out the walk. Add sound effects to match the places she walks by.
- Try changing the order and then retell the story again with the sounds according to the new route.

- Look in the book to find all the preposition words in the story: over, through, etc.
- Create sounds for each of the prepositions in the story.
- Try saying the words in a way that is representative of the action, e.g. – getting higher and then lower for the word 'over'.
- Practise each one with the children.
- Then read the story again while the children make noises or voice sounds at the appropriate words.

Variations

- Alternative titles you could use:
  - *Alfie Weather* by Shirley Hughes; a collection of stories and rhymes about walking in different seasons.
  - *Two by Two and a Half* by David Melling; the nursery class line up for their walk. They hear and see many unusual things.
  - *Daisy and the Moon* by Jane Simmons; the little duck goes on a night-time walk.
  - *The Bear in the Cave* by Michael Rosen; a bear who lives by the sea goes to visit the noisy city.

Chapter 8
Let's cook

Cooking is an excellent way of engaging young children in investigating and exploring their environment, helping them to acquire knowledge and understanding of the world. It encourages them to use their senses and to take notice of changes that occur in some materials. It is also a great time for talking about what they see and hear, and as such is a natural way to develop phonic awareness.

Tip

Healthy eating and good hygiene should always feature in your cooking sessions.

Pizza parade

A tasty way to focus on phonics.

Resources

- Ready-made pizzas or pizza boxes – the ones with pictures of pizzas on them (Activity 1)
- Real or toy food items (Activity 2)
- Ready-made pizza bases (Activities 5 & 6)
- Selection of toppings (Activities 5 & 6)

Activity 1

Aims and objectives

- Listening and remembering alliteration.
- Learning to suggest objects that start with the same sound.

Preparation

- Have a collection of pizzas (wrapped in clear film if you want to eat them later) or pizza boxes that show pictures of the pizza.

What to do

- Show the children some different pizzas. Talk about the toppings. What do they **all** have on them? Cheese!
- What sound does the word 'cheese' begin with?
  /ch/
- Can the children name other foods that begin with /ch/? E.g.
    chips
    chocolate

> chops
> chewy sweets
> Chinese
> chilli
> chicken
> cherries
> chapatti
> chives.
>
> - Which of these could go on top of a pizza?

Activity 2

Aims and objectives

- Tuning into alliteration.
- Learning to make up alliterative phrases.

Preparation

- Collect together some real or toy food items that could be used on a pizza.

What to do

Show the children the foods you have collected. Ask them to identify them, e.g.

> tomato
> mushroom
> pepper
> pepperoni
> sausage
> bacon
> cheese
> olives.

- Tell the children that they are going to work out what some children might like to eat, and what things they don't like.

- Give some examples,
  Thomas likes **t**omatoes
  Megan likes **m**ushrooms
  James doesn't like **b**acon.
- Observe how quickly the children spot the 'rule' about initial sounds.
- Once the 'rule' has been spotted, and everyone understands how the game works, go round the group, each child giving 'likes', and then 'doesn't like' suggestions.

Tip

Make sure you use the initial sound and not the initial letter.

Activity 3

Aims and objectives

- Talking about alliteration.
- Learning to select a range of words that start with the same sound.

What to do

- Play a memory game, collecting foods starting with the same sound.
- Start the game by saying, e.g.
  – 'Megan likes mushrooms.'
- The next child in the circle then repeats this and adds his own suggestion, e.g.
  – 'Megan likes mushrooms and marmalade.'
- Continue around the circle with each child in turn repeating what was said before and then adding another food of his own choice, e.g.
  – 'Megan likes mushrooms, marmalade, mince pies, melon, meringue.'

- – 'Ravi likes radishes, risotto, raspberries, runner beans, rhubarb'
- – 'Chris likes kiwi fruit, carrots, corn-flakes, coconut, corn-on-the-cob.'
- – Use the names of children in your group as far as possible.
- • If two children's names start with the same sound, draw attention to it and link them in the game, e.g.
  - – Nadia and Nisha like nuts, nectarines, new potatoes, naan bread.

Activity 4

Aims and objectives

- • Listening and remembering alliteration.
- • Learning to recall a list of objects that start with the same sound.

What to do

- • Start by collecting lots of appropriate /p/ words so that the children can complete the statement 'My pizza is . . .' e.g.

perfect	poorly
plastic	painted
pink	pale
purple	pongy
pretty	peculiar
a problem	plain
pathetic	poisonous.

- • Then go round the group so that everyone has a chance to repeat the sentence with their own ending – a new /p/ word, one from the collected list, or even a repeat of what someone else said.

Activity 5

Aims and objectives

- • To use language confidently.
- • Learning to ask and respond to questions.

Preparation

- You will need a selection of pizza toppings ready for cooking.
- Ready-made pizza bases.

What to do

- Show the different toppings to the children, naming and identifying each one.
- **Plan your pizza:**
- Use a circular piece of yellow/gold paper for each child, who then draws, colours, paints, or sticks on cut-out pictures of their chosen foods – to design their own pizza.
- **Prepare the toppings:**
- On a clean surface and with appropriate tools and assistance children prepare their own toppings according to their pizza design.
- **Put it together:**
- Arrange the toppings to match their own design.
- Cook and eat.
- During these activities encourage the children to ask questions.
- Start this by asking the children questions such as:
  - What toppings are you using?
  - How many/much will you need?
  - How will you prepare it?
  - What does it feel like?
  - What is this called (tray, knife, etc. as well as the food items)?
  - Why do you think we are using chopping boards?
  - Do we need to wash our hands before we start? Why?

Tip

Use the children's work from the planning stage, and some photographs taken during the activity to create a display.

Activity 6

Aims and objectives

- Listening and remembering environmental sounds.
- Learning to develop vocabulary relating to sounds.

Preparation

- Prepared pizza bases and toppings.

What to do

- As you make pizzas with the children, identify words/sounds to describe what you are doing and what is happening to the food.
- With the children, work out ways to make the sounds yourselves, e.g.

  chopping
  grating
  slicing
  peeling
  cheese bubbling under a grill, pop-pop-pop
  knives clunking down on the chopping boards, clunk-clunk-clunk.

- Use these sounds and activities to adapt 'Peter hammers with one hammer', e.g.
  Nisha chops a mushroom, a mushroom, a mushroom,
  Nisha chops a mushroom,
  Chop, chop, chop.

  Frankie slices tomatoes, tomatoes, tomatoes,
  Frankie slices tomatoes,
  Shlur, shlur, shlur.

- Sing as you work.
- Sing and mime your new song while the pizzas are cooking.

Vegetable soup

Have fun learning and then eat your work!

Resources

- Real or plastic vegetables (Activities 1, 2 & 3)
- A cooking pot – possible a plastic 'cauldron' (Activities 1, 2 & 3)
- Vegetables for making soup (Activities 4 & 5)
- Knives and chopping boards (Activity 4)
- A large saucepan, preferably in clear glass (Activities 3 & 5)

Tip

Sharp knives are safer than blunt ones. One adult to one child and one knife.

Activity 1

Aims and objectives

- Tuning into alliteration.
- Learning to reproduce sounds clearly.

Preparation

- You will need a large stone, some vegetables and a large wooden spoon as well as a large pot – you can sometimes find a plastic 'cauldron' at a garden centre or other outlet selling planters.
- A selection of vegetables – real or plastic.
- When you choose the vegetables for the story try to have some repeat initial sounds, e.g.
   pepper, potato, parsnip, peas (in pods), pumpkin
   tomato, turnip
   carrot, cabbage, cauliflower, kale, corn
   celery, squash, swede, sweet corn, spinach, sprouts
   beans, broccoli, beetroot, butternut squash.

What to do

- Tell the children the story of 'Stone soup', acting it out as you do so.
- Adapt this version to include your vegetables and use any setting of your choice.

Stone soup

A stranger comes to a village looking for shelter and food. The villagers tell him that he can stay with them but that there is no food left, and that they are virtually starving.

The stranger says that he can make soup from a stone, and produces a pot and a stone. He puts the stone into the pot with some water and places it over a fire.

As the stranger stirs the soup he tells the villagers that he once had stone-and-potato soup, and that it was very tasty. One of the villagers goes home and finds a potato that he has left. It is added to the pot.

The stranger then tells them that he once had soup with a turnip in it. One of the villagers goes home, and returns some minutes later with a turnip. The turnip goes into the pot.

[Repeat this scenario with lots of other vegetables.]

Eventually the soup is ready, and everyone in the village has some and declares it very tasty.

The stranger leaves the next day, taking the stone with him.

(**Moral**: great things can be achieved if everyone works together.)

Activity 2

Aims and objectives

- Listening and remembering alliteration.
- Learning to match sounds to objects.

Preparation

- This should be played after you have read the story in Activity 1.

What to do

- Remove the stone from your cooking pot, but keep the vegetables.
- Reach into the pot (keeping it above the children's eye level) and tell them, 'In my soup I have something beginning with . . . /p/'.
- Children guess what it is you have in your hand.
- You may have a pepper, a potato or a parsnip.
- Children can have a turn each, repeating the line, 'In my soup I have something beginning with . . .'

Tip

Remember to use the initial **sound** not letter, and pronounce it as a sound, not by the letter name.

Activity 3

Aims and objectives

- Tuning into oral blending and segmenting.
- Learning to blend words with the same initial phoneme.

Preparation

- Put a selection of real or plastic vegetables in the cooking pot.

What to do

- Reach into the cooking pot and take hold of one of the vegetables, out of the children's sight.
- Ask the children if they can guess which vegetable you are holding.
- Tell them that you will give them a clue.
- Segment the word.

- Who can identify the vegetable?
- Can the children blend the sounds to make the word and tell you the name of the vegetable?
  - 'In my soup I have a p-o-t-a-t-o.'
  - 'In my soup I have a c-a-rr-o-t.'

Activity 4

Aims and objectives

- To use language to enlarge vocabulary.
- Learning to use a variety of action words.

Preparation

- Have a selection of vegetables suitable for making soup.
- You may need to partly prepare some of them to make them manageable for the children.
- You will need knives – so make sure that you have lots of adults available.

What to do

- Chop vegetables into small pieces ready to make soup, placing the pieces in the pan as you go along.
- Talk about colour, smell, texture, etc. as well as the sounds made when preparing the vegetables.
- Make up rhymes as you work.
- Say them later, miming the actions.
- Find a pattern of words that you like, and simply change the name of the vegetable for each new verse, e.g.

Chop the potato, chop, chop, chop,

Keep on going, don't you stop.

Slice the carrot, slice, slice, slice,

When it's cooked it will taste nice.

Peel the turnip, peel it well,

What do you think about its smell?

(Thumbs up or thumbs down according to personal preference.)

Tip

This is a good opportunity to extend the vocabulary of many of the children.

Activity 5

Aims and objectives

- Tuning into environmental sounds.
- Learning to be aware of sounds around them.

Preparation

- Use your chopped vegetables from Activity 4.
- A clear saucepan if possible.
- Access to your kitchen area/cooking appliance.
- And lots of adults!

What to do

- Use your chopped vegetables to make soup with the children.
- Use a large deep pan – clear glass if you can, so that the children look from the side rather than putting their faces above it.
- Encourage the children to be quiet so that they can hear the sounds of the soup as it heats up.
- What sounds does the soup make as it boils?
- Bubble, pop, plop, flump, etc.

Tip

Take care. Watch out for the mixture drying out, hot water and steam!

Recipe

A basic vegetable soup recipe

Fry your chopped vegetables in a little oil for a few minutes until slightly brown.
Add some stock – use some cubes dissolved with hot water.
Leave to simmer until the vegetables are soft – about half an hour. Stir occasionally so that it doesn't stick to the bottom of your pan.
Serve it as it is, or liquidise it when it has cooled a little.
Serve with chunks of bread.

Activity 6

Aims and objectives

- Tuning into sounds we can make.
- Learning to join in with words and actions in songs.

Preparation

- This activity follows on from Activity 5.
- Use the words you have collected during that activity.

What to do

- Work together with the children to adapt 'The wheels on the bus' to sing about soup.
- Remind the children of the sounds they heard when the soup was cooking. Use those words to make up some songs of your own, e.g.
  The soup in the pan goes bubble, bubble, bubble
  bubble, bubble, bubble
  bubble, bubble, bubble
  The soup in the pan goes bubble, bubble, bubble
  All day long.

  The soup in the pan goes pop, pop, pop . . .

  The soup in the pan goes flump, flump, flump . . .

  The children eating soup go mmm, mmm, mmm . . .

- . . . and lots of other sound effects that are too strange to spell but well within the children's ability to repeat!

Jelly on a plate

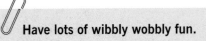

Have lots of wibbly wobbly fun.

Resources

- A copy of the poem 'Don't' by Michael Rosen (Activity 2)
- *Don't Put your Finger in the Jelly, Nelly!* by Nick Sharratt (Activity 2) (Optional)
- Jelly cubes and hot water (Activities 3, 4 & 5)
- Large bowls (Activities 3 & 4)
- Clear plastic tumblers (Activity 5)

Tip

When you plan to do these activities don't forget to allow enough time for the jelly to set.

Activity 1

Aims and objectives

- Tuning into rhythm and rhyme.
- Learning to experience and enjoy rhythm and rhyme.

What to do

- Teach the rhyme 'Jelly on a plate, jelly on a plate':
  Jelly on a plate, jelly on a plate,
  Wibble, wobble,
  Wibble, wobble,
  Jelly on a plate.
- Say it together, with appropriate actions.
- Where else might the jelly be?
- Add some ideas of your own to make new verses.
- It might be:
  in a dish
  in a bowl
  on the floor
  on my spoon
  in my tummy.

Tip

Encourage the children to keep the rhythm as they move.

Activity 2

Aims and objectives

- Talking about rhythm and rhyme.
- Learning to complete sentences using rhyming words.

Preparation

- Have a copy of *Don't* by Michael Rosen.
- Optional: A copy of *Don't Put your Finger in the Jelly, Nelly!* by Nick Sharratt.

What to do

- Read Michael Rosen's poem '*Don't*'.
- Can the children think of any other words that rhyme with 'jelly' (or sound the same as 'jelly')? E.g.
  - Don't put jelly in your welly
  - Don't pour jelly on your belly
  - Don't drop jelly onto Shelley/Kelly
  - Don't buy jelly from the deli.

Tip

Read Nick Sharratt's book *Don't Put your Finger in the Jelly, Nelly!* for even more jelly fun.

Activity 3

Aims and objectives

- To enlarge vocabulary.
- Learning to use descriptive language.

Tip

Make two lots of jelly; one for the children to handle and another made following hygiene rules for the children to eat.

Preparation

- Two sets of jelly cubes and bowls.
- Hot water.

What to do

- Look at the jelly cubes. Let the children handle them.
- Collect words to describe what they feel like, e.g.
    wobbly
    gooey
    squidgy.
- Add hot water to melt them and again collect words to describe what has happened, e.g.
    runny
    watery.
- Now make up the other jelly, with clean hands and no touching, so that you can eat it later. Make sure that you and the children know which jelly is which. Try different colours of jelly or bowl.
- Leave the jellies to set in the fridge.
- Using the first jelly, look at it and handle it. Describe what it is like now, e.g.
    still
    hard
    firm.
- You might want to introduce the terms 'solid', 'liquid' and 'nearly solid'.
- Use the second jelly to collect your last group of words – those that describe what it is like when it is in your mouth!
- Remember to describe the texture as well as the taste.

Activity 4

Aims and objectives

- To speak confidently.
- Learning to ask questions.

Preparation

- Have jelly cubes, hot water and a bowl ready.

What to do

- This activity can be done whenever you are making jelly with the children.
- Encourage the children to ask questions while investigating what happens when jelly is heated up or allowed to go cold.
- Afterwards, identify some of the questions that the children had asked, e.g.
  - 'Why is this happening?'
  - 'What will happen next?'
  - 'When will it be ready?'
  - 'Why are we putting it in the fridge?'
  - 'Why did you have to make the water so hot?'
- Point out to the children that all these 'question' words begin with the sound /w/.
- Can the children think of other question words?
      what
      when
      where
      why
      who
      which.

- Try to think up questions for each of these words in turn.
  - What flavour is the jelly?
  - When will it be cold?
  - Where will we put it to go cold?
  - Why did we put it in the fridge?
  - Who likes red jelly?
  - Which is your favourite jelly flavour?

Activity 5

Aims and objectives

- Tuning into oral blending and segmenting.
- Learning to blend phonemes into words.

Preparation

- Make up lots of different flavours / colours of jelly. These should be cold but not set.
- Provide small transparent containers such as disposable tumblers, one per child.

What to do

- Children choose their first colour of jelly, pour a little into their container and leave it to set in the fridge.
- When it is set add a second and, later, a third colour, leaving it to set each time.
- Once they are set:
- Each child can speak in turn to tell the rest of the group:

  'My rainbow jelly is red, yellow, green.'

- Play a guessing game: Whose jelly am I talking about?
- The adult says:

  'I can see a rainbow jelly that is r-e-d, y-e-ll-ow, g-r-ee-n. Whose is it?'

- Can the children blend the sounds to make the colours and find the owner of that particular rainbow jelly?

Activity 6

Aims and objectives

- Tuning into alliteration.
- Learning to make up alliterative phrases.

Tip

Concentrate on the sounds not the spelling!

What to do

- Ask the children whether they can find some /j/ sounds to describe their jelly?
- See how many ideas they can come up with, e.g.
  'Mine is a . . .'

giant jelly	George jelly
jumping jelly	Jack jelly
jammy jelly	jet jelly
jolly jelly	jewelled jelly
juggling jelly	jiggling jelly
ginger jelly	jumbo jelly
giraffe jelly	jumbled jelly
Gemma jelly	jungle jelly.

- The jewelled jelly could be depicted in paint, collage, etc. to create a display.
- Paint a jelly shape and when it's dry stick on coloured foil 'jewels', or coat it with diluted PVA glue and sprinkle with glitter.

Sandwich time

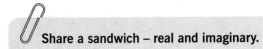

Share a sandwich – real and imaginary.

Resources

- *Sam's Sandwich* by David Pelham (Activities 1 & 2)
- Pictures of food items stuck onto cards (Activity 4)
- Empty lunchbox (Activity 5)

Tip

Start with the super story of *Sam's Sandwich*, by David Pelham, and see where it takes you.

Activity 1

Aims and objectives

- Listening and remembering rhythm and rhyme.
- Learning to be aware of words that rhyme.

Preparation

- Familiarise yourself with the book, *Sam's Sandwich*, by David Pelham.

What to do

- Read the book, *Sam's Sandwich* by David Pelham, to the children.
- As you read it, encourage them to guess what Sam adds each time, by listening for the rhyming word.
  - Sam added to the sandwich!
  - What did he add?
  - Give the children the rhyming word.
- Can they remember what Sam put in?

> need . . . centipede
> hide a . . . spider
> try . . . fly
> squirm . . . worm
> dug . . . slug
> a little filler . . . caterpillar
> pants . . . ants
> trail . . . snail
> a little hole . . . tadpole.

Activity 2

Aims and objectives

- Listening and remembering alliteration.
- Learning to identify the initial sound in words.

Preparation

- Re-read the book *Sam's Sandwich* with the children.

What to do

- What was in the sandwich?

  'There was some . . . in the sandwich.'

- Say the initial sound (not letter) for each item in turn, and help the children to work out the reply:

  /w/ . . . watercress
  /e/ . . . egg
  /t/ . . . tomato
  /ch/ . . . cheese
  /u/ . . . onion
  /s /. . . salami
  /k/ . . . cucumber
  /k/ . . . ketchup.

Activity 3

Aims and objectives

- Listening and remembering alliteration.
- Learning to recall a list of objects that start with the same sound.

> **What to do**
>
> - Play a memory game; all the 'fillings' starting with the same sound, e.g.
>   - Child One: My sandwich has ham
>   - Child Two: My sandwich has ham and honey
>   - Child Three: My sandwich has ham, honey and humus
>   - . . . and so on.
> - Here are some ideas to start with:
>   tuna, tomato, tangerines, toast
>   peanuts, pickle, plums, peaches
>   cheese, chocolate spread, chicken, chilli
>   salad, salami, sausage, celery
>   bacon, beef, beans, banana
>   crisps, carrot, cucumber, cake.

Activity 4

Aims and objectives

- Listening to and remembering alliteration
- Learning to match sounds to objects.

Preparation

- Collect together some pictures of food items. (NO WORDS)
- Make sure that you have an even number of pictures for each initial sound (not spelling!)

honey, ham,	tomato, tuna
sausage, celery	cheese, chips
chicken, chocolate	bacon, beef
beans, bananas	peach, plum
apple, avocado	potato, peas.

- Stick them onto individual cards.

What to do

- Lay the cards face down on the table.
- In turn each child turns over two pictures and says the names of the foods.
- If they begin with the same sound he keeps them 'to make a sandwich'.
- If they begin with different sounds they are turned back over.
- When all the pictures have been paired up, count them to see who has the most 'sandwiches'.

Activity 5

Aims and objectives

- Tuning into rhythm and rhyme.
- Learning to recognise that some words rhyme.

Preparation

- Have an empty lunchbox with you.

What to do

- Hold up your lunchbox and ask the children, 'Can you guess what's in my sandwich today? I'll give you a clue – it rhymes with . . .', e.g.

    'pram' – ham
    'seat' – meat
    'please' – cheese
    'money' – honey
    'Sam' – jam
    'leaf' – beef
    'tickle' – pickle
    'taken' – bacon
    'peg' – egg.

- Repeat this a few times until the children know how this works.
- Ask once more, and the child who answers correctly can come to the front, hold up the lunchbox and ask the next question.
- Continue until everyone has had a turn.

Tip

If you want to focus on initial sounds play it this way: 'Can you guess what's in my sandwich today? I'll give you a clue. It begins with . . . '
(Initial sound, not letter.)

Activity 6

Aims and objectives

- Talking about rhythm and rhyme.
- Learning to create their own rhymes.

What to do

- Choose a familiar tune or rhythm and add your own words to create a 'making a sandwich song' with the children, e.g. to the tune of 'London Bridge is falling down':

Put your bread down on the plate, on the plate, on the plate,

Put your bread down on the plate,

For your sandwich.

Sliced tomatoes go on next . . .

Lay the lettuce on the top . . .

Mayonnaise will taste so nice . . .

Now another slice of bread . . .

Or to the tune of 'Here we go round the mulberry bush':

First of all we'll take some bread, take some bread, take some bread
First of all we'll take some bread,
To make our tasty sandwich.

Then we'll put some cheese on top . . .

Then we'll put some pickle on . . .

Last of all we'll have more bread . . .

Tip

Thinking about alternative words in order to keep the rhythm correct encourages vocabulary development.

Crispy cakes

Fun phonic activities based on this favourite cooking activity.

Resources

- Crispy cereals, bowl, chocolate and paper cases (Activity 1)
- Chocolate and bowl (Activity 4)
- Crispy cakes (Activity 4)
- Dark and light brown sugar paper, fine white paper, foil, a wooden spoon and an empty cereal packet (Activity 5)

Tip

Melt your chocolate in the microwave – it's safer than using boiling water.

Activity 1

Aims and objectives

- Talking about environmental sounds.
- Learning to talk about cooking sounds.

Preparation

- Put some crispy rice cereals into plastic bags.
- Break a bar of chocolate into a microwaveable bowl.
- Have a box of cereals, paper cases and spoons ready.

What to do

- Give the children the plastic bag of cereals and encourage them to really scrunch them.
- Allow time for all of the children to have a turn or use small individual bags.

- Ask the children to describe the sound they made, e.g.
    crunching
    tinkly
    swishing
    scrunch
    crackling
    crisp.

- Now make your cakes.
- Use a fresh supply of cereals for the actual cooking, as you make crispy cakes with the children.
- When you snap the chocolate ready to melt it, see if the children can snap or click their fingers to replicate the sound.
- Continue to collect sound words as you stir the cereals into the melted chocolate and again as you eat the finished cakes.

Tip

Make a note of any words that the children can suggest to describe the sounds they have heard.

Activity 2

Aims and objectives

- Talking about alliteration.
- Learning to select a range of words that start with the same sound.

What to do

- Try describing the crispy cereals with any /k/ sound word.
    'I have a bowl full of . . .', e.g.
    clever crispies
    kind crispies
    careful crispies
    colourful crispies
    crunchy crispies
    crazy crispies
    cooked crispies
    kicking crispies.

Activity 3

Aims and objectives

- Listening and remembering environmental sounds.
- Learning to imitate sounds.

What to do

- You are aiming to mime making the cakes, with sound effects.
- First of all, encourage the children to remember how they made the cakes, getting the process into the correct order.
- Then work out the sounds for:
  - opening the box
  - snapping the chocolate
  - the ping of the microwave when the chocolate is ready
  - stirring in the cereals
  - the fridge humming as it cools them down
  - the noise when you bite into, and eat your cake.
- Make up their own crispy-cake-making routine, making the sounds and action in the correct order.

Variation

- Adult says, 'I can hear someone . . .
  - snapping the chocolate
  - stirring the crispies', etc.
- The children respond with the appropriate action and sound effect.

Activity 4

Aims and objectives

- Tuning into rhythm and rhyme.
- Learning to be aware of rhythm and rhyme in speech.

Preparation

- Use this activity during the cake-making process.

What to do

- When you stir the chocolate admire its smooth, shiny consistency and find words to describe it.
- Use similes, e.g.
  - It's as smooth as . . . silk (satin, ice cream).
  - It's as shiny as . . . a spoon (silver, a mirror, a jewel).
  - It's as dark as . . . night (a black cat, my daddy's coffee).
  - It's as sloppy as . . . soup (jelly, porridge, rice pudding).
- Encourage the children to come up with lots of ideas of their own to complete the similes.
- When the cakes are set encourage the children to describe them, using similes, before they eat them, e.g.
  - My cake is as crunchy as . . . a carrot (a packet of crisps, a stick of celery).
  - My cake is as spiky as . . . a spider (a prickly plant).
  - My cake is as brown as . . . a bear (my hair).
  - My cake is as big as . . . a ball (an apple, an egg).

Tip

If you want to do this as a separate activity, melt some chocolate and then let it cool and set in interesting shapes, and talk about the changes that the children will see.

Activity 5

Aims and objectives

- Speaking confidently.
- Learning to describe their actions in sequence.

Preparation

- If you want to make the display you will need to have dark and light brown sugar paper, fine white paper, foil, a wooden spoon and an empty cereal packet.

What to do

- Allow time for the children to retell how they made the cakes.
- Encourage them to describe the ingredients as well as to remember the order of the procedure.
- Discuss the experience as you help the children to make a display recording the stages of the cooking session, e.g.
  - Folding paper concertina-style to make paper cases.
  - Screwing up paper to make cereals: use pale coloured paper before the chocolate has been added, and dark brown after.
  - Cutting out foil pans.
  - Fixing a real wooden spoon and cereal packet to the display.
  - Making a block of chocolate by drawing black lines on a rectangle of dark brown paper.
- Write the words describing what sounds were heard at each stage in cloud shapes to represent thought or speech bubbles.

Part 5
Physical
development

Chapter 9
Round and round the garden

All early years providers have access to an outdoor play area for the children's physical development. Young children's coordination and control is developed through play that encourages manipulation and movement while using all their senses. The following activities provide opportunities to extend children's speaking and listening skills from playing outdoors.

Playtime

Use children's enthusiasm for outdoor play to focus on phonics.

Resources

- Outdoor play vehicles (Activity 1)
- Small bottles, watering cans, spoons, buckets and jugs in the water tray (Activities 3 & 4)
- Portable tape recorder (Activities 3 & 4)

Tip

The following activities can be adapted to use after gardening, ball games or playing in the sand pit.

Activity 1

Aims and objectives

- Tuning into environmental sounds.
- Learning to be aware of sounds around them.

Preparation

- Get out bikes, toy cars, trolleys, prams, etc.
- Let the children play freely before asking them to listen to sounds.

What to do

- Work in pairs – one standing, the other riding.
- Ask them what sounds they hear as they take turns riding.
- Encourage them to go slowly at first then get faster.
- Ask everyone to stop and tell you about the sounds they heard.
- Think about the clicks and taps as the wheels turn.
- Are they puffing and panting as they pedal?
- Did they make a voice sound when they were speeding along? E.g. – wheeeeeee!
- Now change over so the other child has a turn.

Tip

Make sure everyone changes vehicles every few minutes to keep this fun!

Activity 2

Aims and objectives

- Listening and remembering environmental sounds.
- Learning to imitate sounds they have heard.

Preparation

- Enjoy playing outside with the vehicles being aware of the sounds they have heard.

What to do

- After playing outside sit in a circle with the children.
- Talk about the sounds they identified (see Activity 1).
- Give the children prompts to help them recall how the sounds varied with speed.
- Ask someone to come into the centre of the circle and pretend they are riding one of the vehicles.
- Encourage them to use sound effects as well as actions.
- Can the other children guess what they are riding?
- Are they riding slowly and carefully, or speeding?
- Let the children take turns imitating the sounds and miming the actions.

Tip

To add some extra fun – ask what sounds would you hear if someone crashes or falls off?

Activity 3

Aims and objectives

- Listening and remembering environmental sounds.
- Learning to identify sounds.

Preparation

- You will need small bottles, watering cans, spoons, buckets and jugs in the water tray.
- It will probably be best to work in a small group for these activities.
- The adult needs a portable tape recorder.

What to do

- Tell the children you want to record some sounds they can make in the water.
- Ask them to:
  - Fill the bucket and empty it back into the water.
  - Fill jugs with water then pour them out from different heights.
  - Use the watering can to sprinkle water.
  - Start with empty bottles and push them to the bottom of the filled water tray to fill.
  - Use the spoons to splash and make ripples and bubbles in the water.
- Encourage them to listen to the sounds as you record them.
- When you have returned indoors let the children listen to the sounds on the tape recording.
- Can they identify what is happening to the water?

Activity 4

Aims and objectives

- Talking about sounds.
- Learning to identify sounds that are similar.

Preparation

- Recording of sounds made in the water tray (see Activity 3).
- Collect together the utensils used in the water recordings.

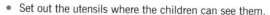

What to do

- Set out the utensils where the children can see them.
- Play a sound and ask who knows what was being used in the water.
- Let a child pick up the utensil and describe what they heard and explain how the sound was made, e.g. I could hear a big swoosh of water as it came out of the bucket.

Activity 5

Aims and objectives

- Listening and remembering sounds we can make.
- Learning to copy a pattern of sounds.

Preparation

- Play on climbing frame before this session.

What to do

- Sit together in a large circle.
- Ask the children to think about the different activities they did on the climbing frame – balancing, climbing, jumping, stretching, swinging, sliding, landing, falling.
- Add actions and vary the way you pronounce each word to demonstrate each activity, e.g.

    Sliding – stretch the word – sl-i-ding – move your arms from high to low.

    Swinging – use a sing-song voice – swing-ing – swinging arms from side to side.

    Jump – say it quickly and clap your hands.

- Tell them you are going to make a pattern of three activities from the climbing frame.
- Watch first, then see if you can copy them.
- List three activities with actions and sound effects, e.g. climb . . . jump . . . swing.
- Ask the children to copy the pattern.
- Repeat with different combinations of activities from the climbing frame.
- The children will soon want to make up their own for others to copy.

Tip

To promote discussion display photographs of the children as they play on the climbing equipment.

Activity 6

Aims and objectives

- Tuning into sounds we can make.
- Learning to join in with words and actions in songs.

Preparation

- Think of sound effects and actions for activities on the climbing frame (see Activity 5).
- Use the tune of 'I went to school one morning and I walked like this'.

What to do

- Remind the children of their different activities on the climbing frame.
- Make the appropriate actions as you sing:

  I played at school one morning and I balanced like this,

  balanced like this, balanced like this.

  I played at school one morning and I balanced like this,

  balanced like this, balanced like this.

  All on the climbing frame.

- Let the children suggest the activities for each verse, e.g.

  swung

  climbed

  jumped.

Tip

The children may need help to use the past tense for the action verbs in this song.

Activity 7

Aims and objectives

- Talking about environmental sounds.
- Learning to talk about sounds they hear.

Preparation

- On a windy day take flags, windmills and kites outside.
- Or make your own structures that will move and create sounds in the wind, e.g. thread small foil containers on lengths of wool.

What to do

- Let the children enjoy running in the wind, feeling it blowing their hair and clothes.
- Give each child something that makes a sound as it moves in the wind.
- Ask them to listen carefully so they can remember their sound and how it was made.
- Return indoors.
- Let the children show what they held in the wind as they talk about the sounds they heard and try to explain how the sounds were made.

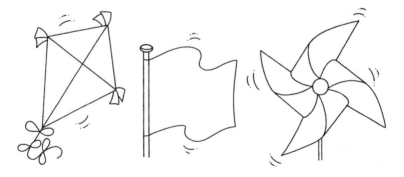

Jasper's Beanstalk by Nick Butterworth and Mick Inkpen

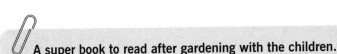

A super book to read after gardening with the children.

Resources

- A copy of *Jasper's Beanstalk* by Nick Butterworth and Mick Inkpen.
- A familiar soft toy with a name.

Activity 1

Aims and objectives

- Listening and remembering environmental sounds.
- Learning to imitate sounds.

Preparation

- You will need a copy of *Jasper's Beanstalk* by Nick Butterworth and Mick Inkpen.
- Set up a screen.

What to do

- Read the story.
- Encourage the children to talk about what Jasper is doing on each page.
- What sounds would you hear?
- Can the children imitate the sounds using hands, feet or voices?
- They may be able to suggest how to make a similar sound with everyday objects in the room, e.g. tapping two bricks together or revving a toy car.
- Choose a sound effect for each illustration in the story.
- Read the story again with children playing the sound effects.
- Set out any objects chosen behind the screen.
- Let the children take turns to hide behind a screen and make a noise from the story.
- Who can guess what Jasper is doing?

Tip

It's fun to read this story when the children are familiar with the traditional tale of *Jack and the Beanstalk*

Activity 2

Aims and objectives

- Using language.
- Learning to make up a new story.

Preparation

- You will need a copy of *Jasper's Beanstalk* by Nick Butterworth and Mick Inkpen.
- A classroom teddy or another favourite toy from the classroom.

What to do

- Read the story *Jasper's Beanstalk*.
- Encourage the children to notice the days of the week as the story unfolds.
- Tell the children you are going to make up a new story.
- Retell the story replacing Jasper's name with one of the toys in your classroom.
- The children will think this is very funny!
- If you have been planting seeds change the bean to the type of seeds you have been planting, e.g. on Monday, Bunny planted a sunflower seed.

Tip

A useful book to help with learning the days of the week.

Activity 3

Aims and objectives

- Listening and remembering alliterative sounds
- Learning to hear the difference in sounds at the beginning of words.

Preparation

- Read the story *Jasper's Beanstalk*.
- A soft toy.

What to do

- Sit in a class circle.
- Can the children remember the name of the cat in the story?

  Jasper begins with /j/

- Tell them you are going to play a game with the classroom toy.
- As you say the days of the week the children pass the toy around the circle.
- When you get to Sunday the child holding the toy says his or her own name.
- Ask if it begins with the same sound as Jasper.
- If not the toy is passed on and you begin again, saying the days of the week.
- If it does begin with /j/, the rest of the children say the child's name as the title of the book, e.g. *Joe's Beanstalk*.
- Everyone gives them a clap!

- N.B. If the child is left holding the toy for a second time ask them to pass it onto the next child.

Tip

On Friday Something Funny Happened by John Prater uses a similar pattern with the days of the week and has great illustrations of lots of noisy activities.

Art in the garden

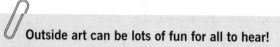

Outside art can be lots of fun for all to hear!

Resources

- Clay, boards and tools (Activity 1)
- A collection of smooth stones in a range of sizes (Activities 2 & 3)
- Paints and brushes (Activities 2 & 3)
- Paper, paints and brushes (Activity 4)
- Collection of dry plant material, elastic bands and ribbons (Activity 5)
- Large sheets of paper, paints and brushes (Activity 6)

Activity 1

Aims and objectives

- Talking about environmental sounds.
- Learning to talk about the sounds made by different materials.

Preparation

- You will need a bag of clay, some boards and tools.

What to do

- Ask the children to listen as you cut the clay.
- What sounds can they hear? *Shluuuurp* – (be inventive!)
- Can the children make the same sounds?
- What else might make a noise like this? E.g.
  - scooping the mixture when cooking
  - digging in the mud.
- As the children handle their clay, encourage them to talk about the sounds they heard. Try:
  - banging the clay on the board
  - slapping two pieces together.

- Use the tools to cut the clay.
- Ask the children to roll the clay to make worms.
- Make patterns on their backs and press in eye shapes.
- As they work encourage everyone to talk about their squiggly, jiggly, wiggly worms!
- When they are finished they could be displayed on a garden flowerbed or hidden in soil for digging up later.

Tip

Extend the children's vocabulary by talking about how the clay feels, how they are creating their worms and comparing their lengths.

Activity 2

Aims and objectives

- Talking about voice sounds.
- Learning to widen the range of vocabulary needed to talk about speech sounds.

Preparation

- Make a collection of smooth stones in a range of sizes.

What to do

- Put the stones together in a large tray.
- Allow the children to push their hands among them and handle them.
- Discuss the sounds they can hear as the stones tumble against one another.
- Ask the children to choose a family of stones.
- Let them choose the size and shape of the stones and how many they want in their family.
- Now suggest that you paint faces on their stones.
- Encourage them to talk about the stones and tell you who's who.
- Let them put them into bags or boxes then give them a gentle shake.

- Can they hear the stones talking?
- What are they saying?
- What kind of voice has the mummy stone?
- Can the baby stone talk properly yet?
- When you have finished this activity the families can be displayed outside in the garden.

Tip

An adult can apply varnish over the paint to make the art work more weather resistant.

Activity 3

Aims and objectives

- Tuning into sounds.
- Learning to experience and enjoy rhythm and rhyme.

Preparation

- Make a collection of smooth stones in a range of sizes.

What to do

- Let the children choose ten stones – one smaller than the others.
- Paint faces on them if you wish.
- Then fit them in a line along the floor and cover them with a scarf as if they were in bed!
- Now sing:
  There were ten in the bed and the little one said – roll over
  So they all rolled over and one fell out.
- Roll one stone from the bed.
- Continue with the song removing one stone with each verse until only the little one is left.
- He can be snuggled up in the scarf – all by himself.
- Goodnight!

Activity 4

Aims and objectives

- Listening and remembering environmental sounds.
- Learning to develop vocabulary.

Preparation

- Large sheets of plain paper outside.
- Secure them down at each corner with masking tape or stones.
- Provide paints and brushes.

Tip

You can do this without rain! Let the children use watering cans and squeezy bottles to wet the paper throughout the activity, if the weather is dry.

What to do

- This painting activity takes place outside in the rain.
- Dress the children for the rainy weather conditions.
- Go outside and sing some rainy weather songs and rhymes:
    'Rain, rain, go away . . .'
    'I hear thunder . . .'
    'It's raining, it's pouring . . .'
    'Doctor Foster went to Gloucester . . .'
- Let the children work in pairs to paint a rainy picture in the rain.
- As they work the paper will be wet and the paint will run and seep together.
- Encourage them to notice the effects of the rain and what it is doing to their painting.
- If possible bring the paintings inside to dry.
- As you look at the paintings together afterwards, talk about the experience.
- Can you tell they were painted in the rain?
- How did they enjoy the painting in the rain? What do they remember?
- What sensations did they feel? What sounds did they hear?
- Are they using any words from the songs you were singing? E.g. thunder / puddle /shower /pitter patter /raindrops /pouring.

Activity 5

Aims and objectives

- Talking about rhyming sounds.
- Learning to make up a series of rhyming words.

Preparation

- Collect some dry plant material.

What to do

- Help the children tie the plant material into bunches with an elastic band and a ribbon.
- As they work, say the rhyme 'Ring a ring of roses' together.
- Play a game of making up words that rhyme with posy.
- There are some real words that rhyme, but nonsense words can be great fun, e.g.

  Rosie
  toesy
  dozy
  mozy
  nosy
  cosy
  bosy
  and all the rest.

- Try saying lots of them together:

  'I've made a cosy, toesy, nosy posy.'

Tip

Encourage competition to see who can make the longest string of rhyming words.

Activity 6

Aims and objectives

- Listening and remembering alliterative sounds.
- Learning to match sounds to objects.

Preparation

- Use masking tape to fix a huge piece of paper round the trunk of a tree, along a fence or wall, or on a pathway.
- Collect together some dry materials ready for your collage work.

What to do

- Children can use wax crayons to make rubbings of the surfaces.
- Lay the rubbings flat. Use diluted paint to paint over the wax for a bright and colourful result.
- When thoroughly dry, provide a selection of materials that start with the same sound as the places you made the rubbings.
- Children can work in groups to find the right place for each material and fix in place, e.g.
  - **Tree**: tinsel, tissue paper, tracing paper
  - **Fence**: feathers, fur fabrics, felt, foil
  - **Pathway**: paper, pasta, petals
  - **Wall**: wool, wallpaper, wax paper.

Noisy sounds

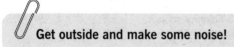

Get outside and make some noise!

Resources

- Poetry book, e.g. *Noisy Poems* illustrated by Debi Gliori
- A selection of beaters, spoons and drumsticks (Activity 3)

Activity 1

Aims and objectives

- Tuning into percussion sounds.
- Learning to recreate sounds with a variety of different rhythms, speed and volume.

Preparation

- Read the poem 'Early in the morning' from *Noisy Poems*.

What to do

- Let the children make the sound of trains/buses/motorboats/ aeroplanes.
- Encourage them to use actions and move around an open space.
- Divide the children into four groups in separate areas of the playground, one for each vehicle.
- As you read the poem they respond with the actions:
  - Stand in a row.
  - Start the engine.
  - Drive around.
- The children can return to their starting point at the end of their verse.

Activity 2

Aims and objectives

- Tuning into percussion sounds.
- Learning to recreate sounds with a variety of different rhythms, speeds and volume.

Preparation

- Read the poem 'Laughing time' by William Jay Smith from *Noisy Poems*.

What to do

- This poem uses lots of different laughing sounds.
- In this game the children will have great fun using these and making up more of their own!
- Sit in a circle and start the game by saying Ho! Ho! Ho!
- The next child must think of a different laughing sound, e.g. Tee! Hee!
- The next child must think of another laughing sound, e.g. Ha! Ha! Ha!
- Carry on round the circle with each child laughing in turn.
- Let the children know they can repeat a laughing sound if they can't think of a new one.
- Go round the circle again, this time with everyone laughing quietly.
- Then try changing the volume to laughing loudly.
- Try changing the speed to laugh slowly or very quickly.
- Have fun!

Tip

Play this outside where all the laughing won't disturb anyone!

Activity 3

Aims and objectives

- Tuning into sounds.
- Learning to experience rhythm.

Preparation

- Read the poem 'City music' by Tony Mitton from *Noisy Poems*.

What to do

- This poem is about tapping out a rhythm and enjoying outdoor sounds in a city.
- Decide on a simple rhythm, e.g. 1-2—1-2-3
- Let the children feel the rhythm by
  - clapping hands
  - tapping their feet
  - moving their arms
  - beeping like a horn
  - tapping on a table.
- Give everyone a spoon or a beater of some kind.
- Go outside and try tapping out the rhythm on bin, door, fence, gate-post, flowerpot, etc.
- Change over beaters so the children experience the sounds made with different materials, e.g. wooden spoons sound different from metal spoons on a metal gate post.
- Enjoy the outdoor music!

Chapter 10
Outdoor fun

Taking your language-based activities outdoors is a good way to integrate phonics into your physical development curriculum. The children will benefit from being active in the fresh air, where they can also take part in sports, dance and movement.

Let's dance

 **Music and dance for action phonics.**

Resources

- Tambourine (Activity 1)
- Coloured streamers or scarves (Activity 1)
- Recording of 'Entrance of the Gladiators' by Julius Fucik (Activity 2)
- Toy robot (Activity 3)
- Tunes for robot dancing (Activity 3)
- A copy of the poem 'Jump or jiggle' from *Is a Caterpillar Ticklish?*
- Selection of music (details set out in Activity 4 preparation)

Activity 1

Aims and objectives

- Listening and remembering voice sounds.
- Learning to listen for a target sound and respond.

Preparation

- You will need a tambourine.
- The children should each have a coloured streamer or fine scarf.
- This is a good dance opportunity for an outdoor session when there's a gentle breeze.

What to do

- Explain to the children that they are going to dance like fireworks.
- Practise the two movements first:
  - Run around to make your streamer trail behind you as the air catches it.
  - Jump up or throw your streamer up, and then catch it before it reaches the ground.

- Play the tambourine by shaking it continually as the children run and trail their streamers.
- Bang the tambourine sharply to indicate that they should jump or throw their streamer.
- Alternate the two sounds and see who is listening carefully.

- The children run around trailing their streamers.
- The adult calls out a colour name.
- The children with that colour streamer jump or throw their streamer once into the air as the others continue to run. Then they continue to run and trail their streamer.

Tip

Make sure everyone is running and trailing before you call the next colour.

Activity 2

Aims and objectives

- Tuning into sounds that we can make.
- Learning to keep in time while moving.

Preparation

- Look at a video clip of a clown or even arrange for one to visit.
- Have a recording of the traditional clowns tune ready: 'Entrance of the Gladiators' by Julius Fucik. You should be able to download this.

Tip

Be aware that some children are afraid of clowns. Check with parents if necessary.

What to do

- Encourage the children to imagine that they are clowns.
- What are you wearing? Funny hat? Red nose? Huge flower in your buttonhole? Big baggy trousers?
- Can you move with flat feet and legs apart – as if you had huge long clown shoes on?
- Can you do this when you are dancing?
- Move around the room like a clown keeping in time with the clown music.
- When you meet another clown pull funny faces at each other. Can you make the other clown smile or laugh?

Activity 3

Aims and objectives

- Talking about instrumental sounds.
- Learning to express an opinion about different musical sounds.

Preparation

- Have some music recorded and ready to play.
- Try the CBeebies website for some suitable music.
- Show the children a battery-operated 'robot' toy. Watch how it moves.

What to do

- Try out some robot moves. Talk with the children about moves which look most like a robot – stiff, jerky movements. Let everyone have another chance to try these out.
- The children are going to dance to several different tunes.

- Afterwards sit round in a circle. Listen to each tune again and choose your favourite. Engage the children in a conversation to find out why they preferred certain pieces.
- Which one sounded most like a robot walking?
- Then play the tunes again and dance along with the music.

Activity 4

Aims and objectives

- Talking about instrumental sounds.
- Learning to develop a wide vocabulary to talk about musical sounds.

Preparation

- Have some music recorded or downloaded and ready to play.
- By using a selection of music for children to dance to you can provide an opportunity for them to talk about different types of music.
- Aim to use a variety of pieces – different speeds, different moods, different types of dance.
- Try to include some traditional and some new pieces of music. Here are some suggestions:

  Slow, heavy music – 'Mars' from *The Planets* by Holst

  Fast, light music – 'The Dance of the Sugar Plum Fairy' from *The Nutcracker* ballet by Tchaikovsky

  Marching music – *The Washington Post* by John Philip Sousa

              – 'Nellie the elephant' comic song

  Comical music – 'The Sting' by Scott Joplin

              – 'The Typewriter' by Leroy Anderson

  Smooth, dreamy waltz – 'The Blue Danube' by Johann Strauss

              – 'The Swan' from *Carnival of the Animals* by Saint-Saëns

  Jolly music – 'The Tritsch Tratsch Polka' by Johann Strauss.

What to do

- Play one of your musical extracts and let the children dance freely, responding to its mood and rhythm.
- Sit round in a group and talk about the music afterwards.
  - What did it make you think of?
  - Was it fast or slow?
  - Was it heavy or light and airy?
  - Was it smooth or jerky?
- Try a different piece of music, dancing to it and then talking about it.
  - Was this music the same as the first one?
  - Was your dance the same or different?
  - Can you describe how it was different?
- Find out as much as the children can tell you about it, and then ask:
  - Which one did you prefer? Why?

Activity 5

Aims and objectives

- Tuning into rhyming sounds.
- Learning to experience and enjoy rhythm and rhyme.

Preparation

- Read the poem 'Jump or jiggle' by Evelyn Beyer.

What to do

- Introduce the poem by telling the children that it is all about the ways that animals move.
- Read the first couplet (two-line verse) and ask the children if they notice anything special about the end words in each line. Say it again, stressing those two words, 'jump' and 'hump'.
- Ask the children to join in as you read it again using the rhyming words as prompts.

- Now think about the movements suggested here.
- Practise a movement for each animal – jumping like a frog, and crawling like a caterpillar.
- Read it again, and let the children do the actions as appropriate.
- Now read the whole poem reading each couplet twice: once for the children to listen and think how they could move, and then again to let them do the movements.

Activity 6

Aims and objectives

- Listening and remembering sounds that we can make.
- Learning to copy and remember patterns of sounds.

Preparation

- You will need some percussion instruments that can make three distinct sounds.
- Try: a tambourine that you can 'shake' and 'bang', and a chime bar that can 'ring'.

What to do

- The children are going to dance a series of three movements.
- To decide on the movements practise listening and responding to each individual sound.
- Shake the tambourine to give a long sound.
- Ask the children to dance to it, e.g. twirling.
- Now bang the tambourine and ask the children to make up a dance step that matches this sound, e.g. leaping.

- Now strike the chime bar. Try to make a tinkly sound that the children can move to, e.g. jiggling.
- Children should be encouraged to make their own choice of movements.
- Now play the three sounds together and ask the children to respond to the sounds with their own dance sequence.
- Change the order each time to encourage the children to listen carefully:

    shake – bang – ring
    shake – shake – ring
    ring – ring – ring
    bang – bang – shake

Tip

You can be as inventive as you want creating your own little dances.

Listen! Who said that?

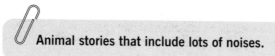

Animal stories that include lots of noises.

Resources

- *Polar Bear, Polar Bear, What Do You Hear?* by Bill Martin and Eric Carle
- *Good-night Owl!* by Pat Hutchins
- *I Don't Want to Go to Bed* by Julie Sykes and Tim Warnes

Activity 1

Aims and objectives

- Listening and remembering sounds that we can make.
- Learning to create sounds for stories.

Preparation

- Enjoy the story *Polar Bear, Polar Bear, What Do You Hear?*

What to do

- Re-read the story and encourage the children to make the different animal noises as you read it.
- Now use a large space so that the children can practise movements that you can make for each of the animals, e.g.
  - Take long slow stealthy steps like a lion following its prey.
  - Stand on all fours with legs and arms as far apart as it is safe to be, and move slowly like a huge hippopotamus.
  - Flap your elbows and walk with high steps like a flamingo.
- Recreate the whole story with the adult as the zookeeper/narrator and the children moving and sounding like the different animals as they appear in the story.

Activity 2

Aims and objectives

- Listening and remembering voice sounds.
- Learning to recognise and identify different sounds.

Preparation

- Have fun reading *Good-night, Owl!*

What to do

- The words chosen by Pat Hutchins suggest very clearly the sounds that the creatures and birds make in this book. As you re-read the story encourage the children to make the sounds of the different creatures as they are mentioned, e.g.

  'the bees buzzed, buzz buzz,
  'the starlings chittered, twit-twit, twit-twit,
  'the jays screamed, ark, ark . . .'

- Sit in a circle. One child comes into the middle and makes one of the noises. Can the others remember or guess which creature it is? The child in the centre chooses someone to guess and if they get it right change places and the game starts again.

- One child sits on a chair pretending to be owl in his tree. He says, 'I can't sleep because I can hear . . .' He names one of the creatures in the story and the other children sitting around the chair/tree have to make that sound. Owl has three 'goes' and then chooses another child to be owl.

Activity 3

Aims and objectives

- Talking about voice sounds.
- Widening the range of vocabulary needed to talk about the different voice and speech sounds they can make or hear.

Preparation

- Read and enjoy *I Don't Want to Go to Bed*.

What to do

- Each of the parent animals that Little Tiger meets speaks in a different way. They roar, growl, bellow, trumpet, and whisper.
- Talk with the children about the different ways that we can speak. We can shout, murmur, whisper, cry, mumble, mutter and whine, and so on.
- Practise saying, 'I don't want to go to bed' in some of these different voices.
- Talk with the children about times when we might use these different voices.
- Remind them of why the monkey whispered.
- Ask them why Mummy Tiger growled – show them the print in the book. It's written very large to suggest how loudly she growled those words.
- Each time Little Tiger goes off in search of a playmate he moves in a different way.
- He scampers, skips, scurries, bounces and tiptoes.
- Listen out for these words and let the children try to move in these ways.
- Read the story again with the children playing the part of Little Tiger, moving as he does – including getting sleepy and lying down quietly to sleep at the end of the story! Try to use different voices as suggested by the words in the story.

Tip

There are lots of other activities you could do from this book. See the ideas in *'Whatever Next'* in Chapter 6, page 157.

Fun in the sun

Things to do on bright days outdoors.

Resources

- Bowls of soapy water, washing line and pegs and some dolls' clothes (Activity 2)
- Ice cubes (Activity 3)

Activity 1

Aims and objectives

- Listening and remembering sounds that we can make.
- Learning to remember patterns of sounds.

Preparation

- Choose a time when the shadows are clearly seen and quite long – early morning or late afternoon.

What to do

- Draw the children's attention to their shadows.
- Move around and watch your shadow.
- Can you make it hop or stretch high or curl up small?
- Once the children have noticed that their shadows copy exactly what they do, tell them that you are going to play a game.
- They will be your shadow. Whatever you do, they must copy.
- Start with simple movements and actions, such as clapping your hands above your head or to the side.
- Then add in some sound effects: 'wheeeee!', or whistle, hum or sing 'la-la'.
- They must copy your sound and the tune or rhythm you have used as well as doing the action.

Tip

This might be something to try in pairs so that the children can watch each other's shadow.

Activity 2

Aims and objectives

- Tuning into environmental sounds.
- Learning to be aware of sounds around them.

Preparation

- Choose a warm day when you can take bowls of soapy water outside and wash the dolls' clothing.
- Have a washing line and pegs available.

What to do

- As the children wash the clothes talk about the various sounds that they are making. They might hear:
  - Water *splashing* in the bowl or onto the ground.
  - Water *dripping* off the clothes as they squeeze them dry.
  - Pegs *knocking* against each other in the basket.
  - Pegs *clicking* as they open them to put them on the line.
- Make up your own washing-the-clothes-song, perhaps to the tune of 'The Farmer's in his Den'.

  Water in the bowl,

  Water in the bowl,

  Splish splash, splish, splash,

  Water in the bowl.

  Squeezing out the clothes,

  Squeezing out the clothes,

  Drip drop, drip drop,

  Squeezing out the clothes.

- Continue to add your own verses and use them at other times with actions to remember the day they did this activity.

Activity 3

Aims and objectives

- Tuning into environmental sounds.
- Learning to describe different sounds.

Preparation

- Have a picnic with the toys.
- Add ice cubes to a large jug of water.

What to do

- Can the children make noises as they pretend to feed the toys?
- Try 'eating', e.g.
    crisps
    carrots
    soup
    ice cream.

- What noises might you hear?
- Listen carefully as you pour out the drinks.
- Talk about what you hear.
- Can you hear the ice cubes clink against each other in the jug?
- Have a jug of ice cubes – no water – and listen to the noise they make when you gently shake the jug.
- Listen again when they have half melted. Is this a different sound?
- What happens when they have completely melted? Do they still make a sound?

Tip

After all the pretence, enjoy eating some of these foods for real.

Activity 4

Aims and objectives

- Talking about rhythm and rhyme.
- Learning to experience and enjoy rhythm and rhyme.

What to do

- Use sunny day songs and rhymes out of doors, e.g.
    'The sun has got his hat on'
    'I have a little shadow' by Robert Louis Stevenson
    'I love the sun'.

- In the poetry collection called *Is a Caterpillar Ticklish?*:
    'Shadow dance' by Ivy O. Eastwick
    'Soap bubbles' by Maisie Cobb
    'Bubble' by Jacqueline Segal.

- Encourage the children to remember the words of some of these.
- Children might enjoy saying their favourite one to the rest of
  the group.

All join in

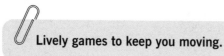

Lively games to keep you moving.

Resources

- Recording device (Activity 3)
- Percussion instruments (Activity 3)

Activity 1

Aims and objectives

- Listening and remembering voice sounds.
- Learning to listen for a target word and respond with an action.

What to do

- How many sports can the children name? For each one work out a movement that represents it, e.g.
  - dribbling a 'ball' for football
  - standing with knees half-bent and arms moving for skiing
  - swinging a racquet for tennis
  - bowling a 'ball' for cricket.
- Name one sport and the children all mime it.
- They keep going until you say another sport.
- Keep changing the sport to keep their interest and try to alternate between actions that are standing still and those that involve moving around the space.
- Alternatively, try letting all of the children mime any sport of their own choice. Whenever you clap (or bang a tambourine if you are in a very large space or outdoors) they have to change to another sport.

Tip

Repeat some of the same sports to help children remember the actions.

Activity 2

Aims and objectives

- Listening and remembering oral blending and segmenting.
- Learning to segment words into phonemes.

What to do

- Explain how cheerleaders support their team by calling out the sounds that make up the name.
- It is really important to remember that at this stage you are not concerned with spelling. Use only the sounds that make up a word.
- Try colour names for your teams.

  /b/ - /l/ - /oo/   (blue)
  /r/ - /e/ - /d/   (red)
  /g/ - /r/ - /ee/ - /n/   (green)
  /p/ - /ur/ - /p/ - /l/   (purple)

- Once the children have mastered two of these divide them into two groups, each cheering for one of the 'teams'. An adult can act as leader, and call out

  'Give me a /b/'   Children reply /b/
  Adult: Give me a /l/   Children: /l/

- And so on through the name.
- At the end the adult says 'What do we have?' And the children say the whole word 'blue'.
- Now the second team can shout out their cheer.
- Once the children can do this, introduce some other colour words without telling them what they are. Go through the calling process, and when you get to 'What have we got?', you will be able to spot which children can blend the sounds back together and hear the right word.

Tip

Add movements to this to increase the fun. Pom-poms are optional!

Activity 3

Aims and objectives

- Tuning into sounds that we can make ourselves.
- Learning to recreate sounds with a variety of different rhythms and speeds.

Preparation

- Have a recording device ready.
- You will need some percussion instruments or shakers for the second part of the activity.

Tip

You will need to do this on a hard surface in outdoor shoes for best effect.

What to do

- The children are going to record their own footsteps. Someone in soft shoes will have to be alongside to make the recording. Their footsteps shouldn't be heard.
- Record lots of different ways of moving, e.g.
    running
    hopping
    skipping
    jumping
    walking.

- Now play back the recording.
- Can the children identify the different ways of moving?
- Hand out some percussion instruments and see if the children can recreate the sounds. Start by playing one sound and letting the children find a good way to recreate it.
- Can they do this movement faster? Or slower?
- Can they play a sequence of sounds such as: run, hop, run?

Part 6
Creative development

Chapter 11
Making and talking

All sorts of creative development activities provide opportunities for phonic awareness. Listening to instructions, describing what you are doing, talking about the work of other artists and making sound effects to go along with your picture or model – these all form part of your phonics programme. We have chosen five pictures that will appeal to young art critics as the starting point for some of these activities. Copies of these pictures are easily available via the internet.

Tip

Enjoy looking at the pictures first before introducing these fun sound activities.

Goldfish **by Henri Matisse**

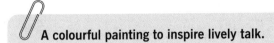

A colourful painting to inspire lively talk.

Resources

- A copy of *Goldfish*
- Plastic bottles (Activity 3)
- Straws (Activity 3)
- Water tray (Activity 3)
- A goldfish in a bowl would be a bonus!

Activity 1

Aims and objectives

- Tuning into voice sounds.
- Learning to distinguish between different vocal sounds.

Preparation

- Show a copy of the picture.
- Encourage the children to look carefully at the picture and point out things they notice.

What to do

- Ask the children what sounds the goldfish are making.
- Encourage them to open and close their mouth like a fish breathing.
- What sounds can you make?
- Can we make the sound of them swimming through the water?
- Make a pattern with the children alternating their sound for swimming and their sound for breathing, e.g.

  woow woow . . . blurrr blurrr . . . woow woow.

Tip

Let the children watch real goldfish swimming in a small bowl.

Activity 2

Aims and objectives

- Talking about alliteration.
- Learning to select a range of words that start with the same sound.

Preparation

- Show a copy of the picture.
- Encourage the children to look carefully at the picture and point out things they notice.

What to do

- Count the fish in the bowl.
- I wonder what their names are? Four fish need four matching names.
- Can we think of four names all beginning with the same sound?
  Remember to use the sound not the letter that the name starts with!
- Try with /f/, e.g.
    Frances
    Fred
    Phoebe
    Fiona.

- Since they are goldfish you might like to try with /g/, e.g.
    Gary
    Gordon
    Grace
    Guy.

- Or choose any sound that the children are familiar with. Try with /j/, e.g.
    Jenny
    Geoffrey
    John
    Judy.

Or /r/, e.g.
    Robert
    Ruby
    Ravi
    Rose.

Tip

Have you read *The Fish Who Could Wish* by John Bush and Korky Paul?

Activity 3

Aims and objectives

- Listening and remembering environmental sounds.
- Learning to imitate sounds.

Preparation

- You will need some small bottles in the water tray.
- It will probably be best to work in a small group for these activities.
- Show a copy of the picture.
- Encourage the children to look carefully at the picture and point out things they notice.

What to do

- Talk to the children about how the fish breathe.
- Then use the bottles in the water tray to demonstrate how the air bubbles rise to the surface of the water.
- Start with empty bottles and push them to the bottom of the filled water tray.
- Show the children how air bubbles rise up when the water is pushed into the bottles.
- Encourage them to listen to the sounds.
- Let the children use straws to blow bubbles into containers of water.
- This is lots of fun and will cause much hilarity!
- But once the initial excitement is over, ask each child in turn to blow while the others listen.

Tip

Have a go at making some bubble prints!
Blow through a straw into paint while holding a piece of paper on top of the container.

The Monkeys by Henri Rousseau

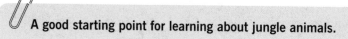

A good starting point for learning about jungle animals.

Resources

- A copy of *The Monkeys*
- *Rumble in the Jungle* by Giles Andreae and David Wojtowycz (Activity 1)
- A video clip of some jungle sounds or a CD of jungle sounds (Activity 1)
- A screen (Activity 1)

Activity 1

Aims and objectives

- Talking about environmental sounds.
- Learning to place sounds in their context.

Preparation

- You will need a copy of *Rumble in the Jungle* by Giles Andreae and David Wojtowycz.
- Or a video clip of some jungle sounds or a CD of jungle sounds.
- Set up a screen.
- Show a copy of the picture.
- Encourage the children to look carefully at the picture and point out things they notice.

What to do

- Talk to the children about the setting of this picture.
- What sounds would you hear if you were in the jungle?
- Listen to the video clip or sound effects of a jungle scene.
- Let them tune into the weird sounds and screeches of the jungle.
- Read the story *Rumble in the Jungle*.
- It is a fantastic rhyming book with loads of jungle noises to join in with!
- The picture invites you into the jungle with its thick, dense undergrowth.
- What might be hiding there?
- Let the children take turns to hide behind a screen and make a jungle noise.
- Who can guess what animal it is?

Tip

An alternative jungle picture is *Surprised!* by Henri Rousseau which shows a tiger.

Activity 2

Aims and objectives

- Tuning into sounds we can make.
- Learning to keep in time.

Preparation

- Show a copy of the picture.
- Encourage the children to look carefully at the picture and point out things they notice.

What to do

- After a discussion about the animals that live in the jungle, use the tune of 'Frère Jacques' to sing a follow-my-leader song:

In the jungle,

In the jungle,

What can you see?

What can you see?

Elephants and monkeys,

Elephants and monkeys,

Tigers as well,

Tigers as well.

- Let the children change the animals included in the song.

Tip

Try singing 'We're going on a tiger hunt' using the ideas in Chapter 6, Explorers.

Activity 3

Aims and objectives

- Talking about alliteration.
- Learning to select a range of words that start with the same sound.

Preparation

- Show a copy of the picture.
- Encourage the children to look carefully at the picture and point out things they notice.

What to do

- Say the word monkey, emphasising the initial sound.
- Ask the children – 'What sound does monkey begin with?'
- Can the children reproduce the initial sound clearly?
- Show the biggest monkey in the foreground and tell them this is Mummy Monkey.
- Can the children suggest names beginning with /m/ for the other monkeys? E.g.
  Mandy
  Mikey
  Myrtle
  Martin
  Megan
  Meena
  May
  Mary
  Mitchell
  Michael
  Marvin.

- Now think about what monkeys like:
  milk
  men
  maps
  mud
  moles
  mints
  mirrors
  money
  moths.

- Take it in turns to say the alliterative phrases using words you have collected, e.g.

  Mandy monkey likes mirrors.

High and wide

Use all three dimensions as you join and combine materials.

Resources

- Autumn leaves, small twigs and seed pods (Activity 1)
- Coat-hangers (Activity 1)
- Netting bags (Activity 1)
- Hoops (Activity 2)
- Feathers (shop bought) (Activity 2)
- String (Activity 2)
- Large cardboard boxes (Activity 3)
- Masking tape (Activity 4)
- Newspapers (Activity 4)
- Pictures of simple sculptures such as 'The Angel of the North' (Activity 4)

Tip

Create your art indoors and outdoors, build it high and wide, and talk phonics as you go along.

Activity 1

Aims and objectives

- Talking about environmental sounds.
- Learning to talk about the sounds made by different materials.

Preparation

- Collect together some natural materials such as dry leaves, small twigs and seed pods, some wire coat-hangers and netting bags.

What to do

- Use sticky tape and fine thread to attach lots of autumn leaves to a coat-hanger to create a mobile.
- Ask the children to listen as you blow on the leaves:
    What sounds can they hear?
    Can the children make the same sounds?
    What else might make a noise like this? E.g.
    - shuffling slippers along a carpet
    - the rain-maker instrument.
- Does the sound change if they put more (or less) leaves on their coat-hanger?
- Would the sound be the same if you tied other objects on to the coat-hanger? Try:
    - small twigs
    - seed heads.
- Provide some net bags – the kind that are used to package oranges, etc.
- Put a few stones in each and suspend them from a coat-hanger.
- What sort of noise does this make?
- Is it louder or softer than the leaf mobile?

Tip

Take the children out to collect twigs, leaves, seed heads, tree bark – anything that has fallen or is dying.

Activity 2

Aims and objectives

- Talking about alliteration.
- Learning to select a range of words that start with the same sound.

Preparation

- Show the children some 'dream-catchers'. These are usually constructed from wood, string or cord and feathers.

What to do

- Tie lengths of string or cord from side to side across a hoop to make a large version.
- Children can add feathers, weaving them in and out of the strings. Use bought feathers in a wide range of colours.
- Talk as you work.
- Can the children suggest other words that start with the same sound as 'feathers'? E.g.
    fluffy
    fine
    fancy
    floating
    fiery
    fragrant
    fussy.
- Use this opportunity to introduce some new words to the children.

Tip

- Wrap a long strip of brown crepe paper round your hoop before you start to make it look like wood.

Activity 3

Aims and objectives

- To enlarge vocabulary.
- Learning to use vocabulary that relates to size and colour.

Preparation

- Use large cardboard boxes, or shoeboxes, securing any flaps with masking tape. Provide large brushes and let the children each paint their own box. Leave them to dry.

What to do

- Together, you create a wall of boxes.

   Talk about the colours.
   Discuss how long it will be or how high.
   Does it look different from the other side?

- Useful vocabulary to introduce:
   wide
   narrow
   high
   short
   long
   colourful
   bright
   cheerful
   exciting
   huge
   enormous.

- Develop these words into phrases or descriptions, e.g.
   It looks like Elmer the elephant.
   It's like a huge picture.
   Perhaps Humpty Dumpty sat on a wall like this.

- Change the boxes around and talk about the differences this creates.

Tip

- Take digital photographs of each variation and make a display of these.

Activity 4

Aims and objectives

- To talk about environmental sounds.
- Learning to describe the sounds that occur as they manipulate paper.

Preparation

- Use sheets of newspaper.
- Roll them up tightly.
- Secure them with masking tape.

What to do

- As the children prepare their paper rolls talk about the sounds that they make, e.g.
    tearing
    ripping
    scrunching.

- What noise do you hear as the masking tape is unrolled?
- Children may be able to replicate some of the noises they hear.
- Children will use the rolls to make structures.
- Look at a picture of 'The Angel of the North'. Talk about how to recreate it.
- As they work with the rolls what noises can they make? E.g.
    shaking the rolls
    knocking them against each other as they combine them.

- Embellish your structure as appropriate, e.g.
    add a box underneath it as a plinth
    add features to the head to give it a face.

Tip

Make rolls in different lengths and different thicknesses so that you can be creative in the structures you will make with them.

The Great Wave by **Katsushika Hokusu**

An appealing print showing a huge crashing wave!

Resources

- A copy of *The Great Wave*
- Outdoor water tray (Activity 1)
- Small plastic trays with deep sides (Activity 1)
- Tape recorder or other way of recording sounds (Activity 1)
- Video clip of the sea with crashing waves (optional)
- Drum or tambourine (Activity 2)

Tip

Talk to the children about their experience of the sea.
Have they paddled in the sea and jumped over small waves?
If not try to provide some outdoor fun in a paddling pool.

Activity 1

Aims and objectives

- Talking about environmental sounds.
- Learning to talk about the sounds of the sea.

Preparation

- This is best done outside so that you can have lots of fun with the water tray.
- Show a copy of the picture.
- Encourage the children to look carefully at the picture and point out things they notice.

What to do

- Talk about the wave.
- How big do they think the wave in the picture is?
- What sounds would you hear if you were in the picture?
- Tell the children they are going to make waves.
- Let them play with small trays of water – rocking them to produce waves.
- Let them tip the water into the big water tray and listen to the crash.
- Record the sounds.

Tip

Find a video clip of the sea on the internet and listen to the sound of waves crashing.

Activity 2

Aims and objectives

- Listening and remembering instrumental sounds.
- Learning to discriminate between loud and quiet sounds.

Preparation

- Have a selection of instruments available, including a drum or tambourine.
- Show a copy of the picture.
- Encourage the children to look carefully at the picture and point out things they notice.

What to do

- Talk about how the wave gets bigger as it rolls.
- Encourage the children to make a rolling motion with their arms that starts small and grows larger and larger until it crashes.
- Introduce a drum or a tambourine.
- Ask the children to make a quiet sound grow gradually louder and louder.
- Then end with a big crash.
- Let the children choose other instruments to play and record their wave sound effects.
- Play their sound effects while looking again at the picture.

Activity 3

Aims and objectives

- To use adjectives.
- To describe the wave in the picture.

Preparation

- Show a copy of the picture.
- Encourage the children to look carefully at the picture and point out things they notice.

What to do

- Talk to the children about the title of the picture.
- Why do they think the artist chose that title?
- Ask if anyone can think of a different word to describe the wave.
- They may suggest words that describe the size of the wave, e.g.
    the big wave
    the enormous wave.

- Look again at the picture and try to think of other characteristics, e.g.
    the special wave
    the frightening wave
    the beautiful wave
    the foaming wave.

- How many different ways can you think to describe the wave?

Variations

- You can ask the children to think of words that begin with /w/, e.g.
    the wide wave
    the wet wave
    the wonderful wave . . .

- Other /w/ words:
    wobbly
    white
    wishing
    wicked
    worst
    whispering.

Tip

This picture is a print. Get out the finger paints and create some crashing waves on the table. Lay a piece of paper on the wet paint and then lift it off to reveal a print.

Who's behind there?

 Have fun with puppets and masks.

Resources

- Wooden spoons (Activity 1)
- Paper bags (Activity 1)
- Oddments of fabric and wool (Activities 1, 2 & 3)
- Socks (Activity 2)
- Paper plates (Activity 3)
- Pot-plant canes (Activity 3)
- Large cardboard boxes (Activity 4)
- Buttons, lids (Activity 4)
- Ready-made puppets (Activity 5)

Tip

A visit from a puppet theatre group would be a good starting point for this work.

Activity 1

Aims and objectives

- Talking about alliteration.
- Learning to select a range of words that start with the same sound.

Preparation

- Use wooden spoons and paper bags to make simple puppets.

Tip

Children can draw a face onto the bowl of the spoon using felt-tipped pens, and stick on wool or paper curls for hair or beard. Push the handle through the bottom of a paper bag to form a 'dress' and secure with thread or an elastic band.

What to do

- As you work, talk about the names you will use.
- Decide on a family name first: 'Woodenheads' is a good description, but be as inventive as your children can manage.
- Now, everyone has to come up with a name that starts with the same sound as your chosen family name, e.g.
  William Woodenhead
  Winnie Woodenhead
  Wacky Woodenhead
  Whiskery Woodenhead
  Wobbly Woodenhead.

- Use the family of puppets to recreate stories, using props from your small world toys.

Activity 2

Aims and objectives

- Listening and remembering voice sounds.
- Learning to listen for a target word and respond with associated sound.

Preparation

- Ask everyone to bring in an old sock. Socks with longer legs are better than ankle socks for this activity.

Tip

Children can use ready cut scraps of felt to add features to make an animal of their choice.

What to do

- Make up a story in the style of *Dear Zoo*, by Rod Campbell.

    I wanted a new pet.
    The zoo/farmer/pet shop owner sent me a . . .
    (Child makes noise)
      It was too noisy, so I sent it back.

- Use the animals that the children have made. The child with that puppet makes the noise of that animal when the 'crate' is opened.

Activity 3

Aims and objectives

- Talking about voice sounds.
- Learning to widen the range of vocabulary needed to talk about the different voice and speech sounds they can make or hear.

Preparation

- Each child needs two paper plates and a thin pot-plant cane.
- Use sticky paper to make a happy face on one plate and a sad face on the other.
- Stick them together with the cane in between, then add hair.

Tip

You can buy packets of these green canes at DIY outlets as well as in garden centres.

What to do

- Read or tell a story of a child or animal that has lost something, or someone.
- What would the voice be like, what would the expression look like?
- Children can work in pairs to show their friend which side of their puppet is best.

- They can try out different voices to say the words used by the character.
- Discuss with the children what those voices sounded like, e.g.
    whispering
    nearly crying
    long, drawn-out sounds as they called the name.

- Now talk about what happened when they found their missing toy or friend.
- Which face, what sort of voice?
- What differences were there on these two occasions?
- Retell the story with the children saying the words and showing the faces in appropriate ways.

Activity 4

Aims and objectives

- Listening and remembering sounds in words.
- Learning to segment words into phonemes.

Preparation

- Each child needs to make a 'robot head' that he can put on.
- Prepare some cardboard boxes that are big enough to go over a child's head.
- Cut out a rectangular hole (shaped like a letter box) for the child to look out of.
- Children can paint these and decorate them with buttons for knobs, dials, etc.

What to do

- Tell the children that when they have their robot head on they have to speak in a different way. They have to say the sounds that make up the words.

- Demonstrate with a simple instruction or sentence, e.g.

p-u-t	u-p	y-our	h-a-n-d
s-i-t	d-ow-n		
s-t-a-n-d	u-p		
l-ie d-ow-n			
kn-ee-l			
h-o-p			
w-al-k	o-n	t-i-p-t-oe.	

- Can the children give any of these instructions to the other robots?

Tip

Leave these out for the children to play freely. They may continue to practise segmenting words into sounds!

Activity 5

Aims and objectives

- Listening and remembering voice sounds.
- Learning to recognise and identify different voices.

Preparation

- Use your puppet theatre, or a table draped with a cloth so that the puppeteers can't be seen by the audience.

What to do

- In pairs the children go behind the theatre, choose a puppet each and in turn perform a nursery rhyme or song to the audience.
- When they have finished the audience has to decide which child was holding which puppet.
- Can they recognise their friends by their voices?

The Visitor by Arthur Hopkins

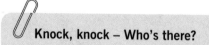

Knock, knock – Who's there?

Resources

- A copy of *The Visitor*
- Mobile phone ring tones (Activity 1)
- Audio clip of doorbells and ring tones (Activity 1)
- A screen (Activity 2)

Activity 1

Aims and objectives

- Listening and remembering environmental sounds.
- Learning to develop a vocabulary to talk about sounds.

Preparation

- Have a selection of ring tones from mobile phones.
- Show a copy of the picture.
- Encourage the children to look carefully at the picture and point out things they notice.

What to do

- Talk about what sounds you would hear if you were in the picture.
- Encourage the children to knock on different surfaces in the room.
- Talk about the sounds they hear on surfaces such as:
  wood
  plastic table
  carpet
  cardboard box
  plastic box
  metal radiator.

- Can they see the doorknocker on the door in the picture?
- How does it work?
- Why is it there?
- What do they have on their front door?
- Some children might be able to recall the sound of their particular doorbell.
- Ask the children about other ways people contact us and the sounds we might hear.
- Play the children some ring tones from doorbells and mobile phones.
- The children might even recognise some of them.
- Talk about which ones they like best and which are most effective.

Tip

What about knock knock jokes? Do they know any? Teach the children a few simple ones e.g. Knock knock – Who's there? Doctor – Doctor who? You just said it: Doctor Who!

Activity 2

Aims and objectives

- Tuning into voice sounds.
- Learning to distinguish between differences in vocal sounds.

Preparation

- Set up a screen.
- Show a copy of the picture.
- Encourage the children to look carefully at the picture and point out things they notice.

What to do

- Ask the children – Who is the little girl coming to visit? E.g. her grandma.
- Expand their suggestions by asking does this remind the children of any stories they know? E.g. *Little Red Riding Hood.*

- Stand behind the screen and ask a child to knock on the pretend door of the screen.
- Change your voice as you have a conversation through the door as if you are the child's grandma.
- Let the children take turns speaking the parts.
- Thinking of different people who might live in the house will create different voices.
- The girl could be visiting her teacher or a friend, her grandfather, a witch, a giant, etc.

Variation

- Make up a story about the little girl, including her journey, who she is visiting and what happens next.

Activity 3

Aims and objectives

- Listening and remembering rhyming sounds.
- Learning to repeat a rhyming string.

Preparation

- Show a copy of the picture.
- Encourage the children to look carefully at the picture and point out things they notice.

What to do

- With the children, think of words that rhyme with knock, e.g.
  lock
  sock
  frock
  flock

shock
rock
mock
tock
dock
chock
spock.

- When you have found lots of words sit in a large circle and take it in turns to knock on the floor twice then say a rhyming knock word. The children could use one of the suggestions or could even invent a 'word' of their own.

Tip

Read the book *Who's There?* by Anthony Browne – it's a super book on the same theme.

The Cholmondeley Sisters – artist unknown

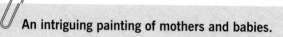

An intriguing painting of mothers and babies.

Resources

- A copy of *The Cholmondeley Sisters*
- Small cards for writing on (Activity 1)
- Two baby dolls (Activity 1)
- Cardboard smiley face and sad face (Activity 3)

Activity 1

Aims and objectives

- Tuning into alliteration.
- Learning to identify the initial sound in words.

Preparation

- Think of names for the mothers, e.g. Lucinda and Esmeralda.
- Make two sets of cards with one name written on each card – use the same initial as the mothers, e.g. if you choose Lucinda and Esmerelda for the mothers you will need a set of names beginning with E and another set of names beginning with L.
- Show a copy of the picture.
- Encourage the children to look carefully at the picture and point out things they notice.

What to do

- Talk to the children about the babies in this picture.
- Are they a boy and a girl?
- Have they noticed that the mother's dress matches the dress of her baby?
- Maybe she would also want her baby's name to start with the same sound as her name.

- Two children can be chosen to be the mothers and sit at the front.
- They need to remember and repeat their name – the mother's name!
- Give each child a baby to hold.
- Read out two cards with names beginning with each mother's name, e.g.

   Lucy and Elroy
   Emily and Lawrence
   Lenny and Edward
   Elliot and Linda
   Lily and Elvis
   Eric and Louise.

- Can the children match the baby's name to the correct mother's name?
- If so they take the name card and give it to the mother.
- When all the cards have been given out see how many baby names the children can remember.
- The child who is playing Mother can choose one of the names you have listed to name her baby.

Tip

The babies in the picture are probably not twins – can the children explain why not?

Activity 2

Aims and objectives

- Listening and remembering sounds we can make.
- Learning to copy a pattern of sounds.

Preparation

- Show a copy of the picture.
- Encourage the children to look carefully at the picture and point out things they notice.

What to do

- The mothers and babies look identical in this picture.
- Introduce the word identical to the children and tell them that you want them to try to make a sound identical to the one you make.
- Make a series of three taps and claps – using your fingers, hands or feet.
- Can the children copy the pattern?
- Try using your tongue and lips to create different body sounds.
- Once they have the idea you can vary the rhythm, speed or volume of the sounds in the pattern.
- Let the children take turns making up a sound pattern for others to copy.

Tip

Try playing spot the differences with the picture.

Activity 3

Aims and objectives

- Talking about sounds we can make.
- Learning to group sounds by a given criteria.

Preparation

- You will need a cardboard smiley face and a sad face.
- Show a copy of the picture.
- Encourage the children to look carefully at the picture and point out things they notice.

What to do

- Talk about what sounds you would hear if you were in the room with these babies and their mothers.
- Show the children the smiley face.
- Ask them to make any sounds the babies would make when they were happy.

- Praise the children for making a variety of different quiet gurgling sounds.
- Now show them the sad face.
- Ask what sounds we'd hear if the babies weren't happy.
- Encourage a range of soft sobbing sounds.
- Now think about what sounds we might hear from the mothers as they comfort the babies.
- Finally, what sounds would we hear when the babies are sleeping?
- Choose individual children to make a sound from the picture and ask another child if it's a happy baby, a sad baby, a sleeping baby or a mother.

Tip

A lovely picture to use during a theme about babies.

Chapter 12
It's showtime!

Phonics can be an additional activity when you are making music with the children as part of their creative development. You may be making music with instruments that you have made, with noisy objects that you've found or using real instruments.

Drama is another aspect of creative development. Children love dressing up and acting out familiar stories. Many traditional tales use memorable language patterns that help develop children's phonic awareness. We have chosen five traditional fairy stories that lend themselves to drama activities. Choose a book with good quality illustrations and dialogue to inspire the children.

Tip

When the children are familiar with several stories see if they can identify which dialogue is from which story and which character speaks those words!

Instrumental differences

Have fun listening for different sounds.

Resources

- Percussion instruments (Activities 1 & 3)
- Chime bars (Activity 5)
- Coloured paper (Activity 5)
- Coloured sticky labels (little circles or rectangles) (Activity 5)
- A collection of everyday objects that make noises (suggestions listed in Activity 4)

Activity 1

Aims and objectives

- Talking about instrumental sounds.
- Learning to match sounds to instruments.

Preparation

- Provide four bought instruments that produce distinctive sounds.
- Four shakers with distinctive sounds can be used as an alternative.

Tip

Check that the children can name the instruments and have heard them before you start the actual activities.

What to do

- Place all the instruments out of sight.
- Play one of them.
- Remove the 'screen' and ask the children to identify the one you played.
- Test their suggestions to confirm their choice – or not!

- You will need two of each of your four chosen instruments: one for a child and one for you.
- Each child has one instrument. The other instruments are placed out of sight.
- You play one, out of sight – and the child who has that instrument plays his back to you.
- Did the child get it right?
- Play yours again, along with the child and let the others confirm or not.

Variation

- Play these two games using four shakers with different contents.

Activity 2

Aims and objectives

- Listening and remembering instrumental sounds.
- Learning to discriminate between loud and quiet sounds.

Preparation

- A small group of children have an instrument each.
- With the children, agree signals for *getting louder* and *getting quieter*.

What to do

- The children sing and play a given song or nursery rhyme.
- The adult acts as conductor and controls the volume using the agreed signals.
- Who is watching and responding?
- Let each child in turn be the conductor.

Tip

Include this activity in any of your singing sessions.

Activity 3

Aims and objectives

- Listening and remembering instrumental sounds.
- Learning to discriminate between loud and quiet sounds.

Preparation

- A small group of children sit in a circle, with an instrument each.

What to do

- – First child plays a short rhythmic pattern on his instrument very quietly.
  - Second child then plays the same pattern on his instrument, but a little louder.
  - Third child plays it loudly.
  - Fourth child, a little quieter.
  - Fifth child plays quietly.
- The pattern continues all round the circle for as long as you can keep it going, with the sound rising and falling like a Mexican wave.

Tip

Decide on a simple rhythmic pattern before you try this the first time so that the children know when to start and finish their own turn. Children will eventually be able to be more spontaneous, simply taking over from the child when he stops.

Activity 4

Aims and objectives

- Talking about instrumental sounds.
- Learning to use sound in imaginative ways.

Preparation

- Collect together some objects that make sounds, e.g.
  - a pen that can click on and off
  - a toy robot
  - an ornamental hand bell
  - a bunch of keys.
- Add these to your music table.

What to do

- Tell a story or read a poem.
- *Choo Choo Clickety Clack* by Margaret Mayo and Alex Ayliffe would be a suitable choice as it includes lots of mechanical sounds.
- Let the children choose things from the table to act as sound effects.
- Ask them to explain their choices.
- Now read the story again with the sound effects.

Activity 5

Aims and objectives

- Talking about instrumental sounds.
- Learning to use sound in imaginative ways.

Preparation

- Cut some strips of paper in three different colours.
- Have some sticky labels in the same three colours.
- Each child chooses three chime bars.
- The child sticks a differently coloured label onto each of his three chime bars.

Tip

Let the children experiment with different combinations of chime bars until they find a set that they like.

What to do

- Working as a group the adult holds up one colour strip and the children all play the matching chime bar in their set. Do this with each colour in turn in any order.
- Repeat in a random fashion.
- Stick several strips up and point to them in order, left to right. The children play their chime bars as you indicate.
- Working individually or with a friend children can create a short pattern of sounds and record it by arranging the coloured strips in the order they played their chime bars.
- On a large sheet of paper, each child can stick down the coloured strips (or use more sticky labels) in the pattern of their tune. Share your music with a friend. Try playing someone else's tune. If the children have different notes on their chime bars the results will always sound different.

Jack and the Beanstalk

Tell this story and use these drama activities when you are growing beans in the classroom.

Resources

- Waistcoat for Jack
- Headscarf for mother
- Hat for old man
- Pull-along toy animal for cow

Activity 1

Aims and objectives

- Tuning into differences in voice sounds.
- Learning to distinguish between different vocal sounds.

Preparation

- Read the story to the children using different voices for each character.

What to do

- Talk to the children about the beginning of the story when Jack is sent to market to sell their cow – remind the children that Jack's mother is worried and ask what she might say to Jack.
- Then talk about Jack and how he feels as he sets off (he's confident and optimistic).
- Ask what they know about the old man and what sort of voice he would use. (Is he a magician?)
- Encourage the children to use three distinct voices as they take turns saying a simple sentence for the characters.
- Let the children take turns to act out the first part of the story finishing when Jack's mother throws the beans away in disgust and Jack is sent to bed without any supper.

Activity 2

Aims and objectives

- Tuning into rhythm and rhyme.
- Learning to be aware of rhythm and rhyme in speech.

Preparation

- Read the story to the children.
- Help the children to remember the things that Jack took from the giant, and the order of this in the story version you are using.

What to do

- Let all the children walk around acting like the giant. Encourage them to say the rhyme 'Fee Fi Fo Fum – I smell the blood of an Englishman', using a giant's voice.
- Tell the children to sit down and pretend to count their money then fall asleep. What sounds would the giant make as he slept?
- Now encourage them to move quickly and secretively like Jack when he climbed the beanstalk and crept up on the sleeping giant. If possible act out this part of the story in pairs with one child being the giant and the other being Jack. Repeat the actions to show Jack stealing the coins, hen and golden harp.
- End the drama with Jack chopping down the beanstalk – let all the children make chopping noises as they pretend to chop then cheer and clap when their beanstalk crashes down!

The Three Little Pigs

Activities that fit in well when you are exploring unusual materials.

Resources

- Three pig masks
- Straw
- Sticks
- Bricks
- Wolf ears

Activity 1

Aims and objectives

- Tuning into rhythm and rhyme.
- Learning to be aware of rhythm and rhyme in speech.

Preparation

- Read the story to the children encouraging them to join in with the repeating rhymes:

  Little pig, little pig let me come in.
  No, no, by the hairs on my chinny-chin-chin, I will not let you in.
  Then I'll huff and I'll puff and I'll blow your house in.

What to do

- Put out a pile of straw, a pile of sticks and a pile of bricks.
- Choose three children to be the three little pigs, let each one make a house by making a circle with the material then sitting inside the circle.
- Choose a child to be the wolf who stands outside each circle in turn for the exchange of dialogue, 'Little pig . . .' etc.
- The first two pigs escape into the third house and then they all say, 'Go away, Mr Wolf – this house is made of bricks and we won't let you in!'
- The wolf walks away and the pigs celebrate!

Activity 2

Aims and objectives

- To develop language.
- Learning to devise and ask relevant questions.

Preparation

- Set out a special chair for the 'hot seat'.
- Have a selection of dressing-up clothes for the characters in the story.

What to do

- One person at a time dresses up as one of the characters and sits in the 'hot seat'.
- The others ask questions and the person in the 'hot seat' has to answer in character. Encourage the children to use an appropriate voice and to think about things from the perspective of the character.
- Questions might include:
  Where did you get your straw/wood/bricks from?
  Why did you choose that material for building your house?
  What is your name?
  Were you frightened when the wolf came to your door?
  Do you think pigs and wolves can be friends?

Tip

An adult may need to demonstrate this process by being the first one to dress up and sit in the 'hot seat'.

Shake it, baby!

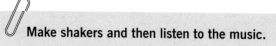

Make shakers and then listen to the music.

Resources

- Plastic water bottles, filled with dry rice, dry pasta, gravel, sand, dry peas or beans – tightly sealed (all activities)
- Paper bowls or spare bottles (Activity 5)

Activity 1

Aims and objectives

- Listening and remembering instrumental sounds.
- Learning to discriminate between loud and quiet sounds.

Preparation

- Sit in a circle with a shaker each.

What to do

- Practise making loud sounds, and then quiet sounds with your shaker. Talk about how you are doing this. Which sort of movement makes a quiet sound, and, which makes a loud one?
- Play a ring game:
    You play loud, the child next to you on your left plays quietly.
    The child to his left then plays loudly.
- Continue in this alternating pattern round the circle. Try to keep it going.

Tip

Have an odd number of people in your circle so that each child gets a turn at loud and quiet sound making.

Activity 2

Aims and objectives

- Tuning into instrumental sounds.
- Learning to respond to musical sounds.

Preparation

- Sit in a circle with a shaker each.
- Test out your shakers by playing them:
    loud or soft
    fast or slow
    or any combination of these.

What to do

- You play a short, clear rhythm.
- The next child in the circle repeats it, as does each other child in turn.
- If you play quietly, so must the children.
- When it has been round the circle and it is your turn again, play a different tune and, again, everyone repeats it in turn.
- Vary the volume as well as the rhythm each time, and try to keep the music going.

- Once the children can do this, make it a little trickier.
- Have a signal, such as a bell played by another adult in the room, but not in the circle.
- When they hear the bell, whoever's turn is next must change the rhythm, and everyone will follow this new rhythm.

Activity 3

Aims and objectives

- Talking about instrumental sounds.
- Learning to use sound in imaginative ways.

Preparation

- Have a collection of shakers with different contents.

- If you have used transparent bottles the children will be able to choose easily.
- To make it harder wrap paper round the bottles.

What to do

- Ask the children: Can you find a shaker that sounds like . . .
  a rain shower
  a thunderstorm
  walking on sand
  walking on gravel
  crunching crisps?
- A child comes to the front, tests the shakers and then chooses the one that he thinks is the best match.

Activity 4

Aims and objectives

- Talking about instrumental sounds.
- Learning to use sound in imaginative ways.

Preparation

- Each child has a shaker. The contents of the shaker don't matter for this activity.

What to do

- Tell the children, 'I can hear a mouse . . . walking.'
- The children play their shakers to represent the sound or action of walking.
- The mouse could then be heard to
  stamp
  run
  jump
  dance
  hop
  shuffle
  with the children making up suitable sounds and rhythms.

Activity 5

Aims and objectives

- Listening and remembering instrumental sounds.
- Learning to identify the differences between the sounds of different instruments.

Preparation

- You will need five shakers.
- Make a set of five shakers that are opaque but identifiable. You could wrap some tape in different colours round water bottles that have been covered in paper.
- You need to be able to open up the shakers.
- Take five different fillings and place one type in each bottle, e.g.

  a cube
  some sand
  some pasta
  a pencil
  some small stones.

- Keep a little of each filling to use later.
- Don't let the children see you do this.

What to do

- Line up the shakers and let the children hear the sounds they make.
- Can they identify what is in each bottle?
- Now show them the other set of the contents. These can be in a second set of clear bottles or in paper bowls. Ask them to identify which of these objects made which sound. Show them, for example, a cube, and ask them which shaker it is in. Let them test the shakers to find out.
- Swap the contents round, out of sight, and let them try again.

Goldilocks and the Three Bears

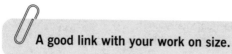

A good link with your work on size.

Resources

- Ribbons for Goldilocks
- Three bowls, chairs and beds (use towels or small blankets to represent the beds) in three sizes
- Three bear masks

Activity 1

Aims and objectives

- Tuning into voice sounds.
- Learning to articulate words carefully.

Preparation

- Read the story to the children, encouraging them to join in with the repeating parts:

    Who's been eating . . .

    Someone's eaten . . .
- Arrange the three bowls, three chairs and three 'beds' together in an area representing the cottage.
- Choose three children to be the three bears and someone to be Goldilocks.

What to do

- Introduce the drama by saying: 'Mummy Bear has made the porridge for breakfast but it's too hot so the bears leave it to cool and go out for a walk.'
- The three bears walk out together and sit at the side.
- Goldilocks comes into the cottage and tries the porridge, the chairs and the beds, finally falling asleep on the smallest bed.

- When the three bears come back to the cottage they speak their words, e.g.

  Baby Bear: Someone's been eating my porridge . . . and they've eaten it all up!

- The drama ends when Goldilocks runs out of the cottage.

Activity 2

Aims and objectives

- Tuning into sounds they can make.
- Learning to join in with words and actions in songs.

Preparation

- Have a selection of instruments available.

What to do

- Spend time with the children choosing three instruments to represent the three sizes in the story. Test all of their suggestions until you have three suitable instrumental sounds, e.g.

  the largest drum you have for 'large'
  a tambourine for the 'medium-sized'
  a triangle for 'small'.
- Now sing *'When Goldilocks came to the house of the bears / What did her blue eyes see?'*
- As you sing '1, 2, 3' each verse, play the appropriate instruments.

  1 = large
  2 = medium
  3 = small.

Here comes the band!

Have lots of fun making your own instruments.

Resources

- Junk materials: boxes, tubes, yoghurt pots, sticks.
- String, elastic bands, glue, masking tape.

Aims and objectives

- Talking about instrumental sounds.
- Learning to develop a wide vocabulary to talk about musical sounds.

Preparation

Set out your 'making table' with junk materials and suitable fixings. You may need to demonstrate some of the methods to create musical instruments by making some instruments yourself first.

What to do

- Make instruments that you can beat, shake or pluck.
- Ask questions as the children work, helping them to see that different instruments are played in different ways:
  - Shakers made from pots or plastic bottles need to be shaken.
  - Drums made from covered tins (stretch strong paper or fabric over and hold in place with an elastic band) need to be beaten.
  - Guitars made from elastic bands stretched over the hole in a tissue box need to be plucked.
- Once you have a lot of instruments made, the children can march around the grounds singing and playing. Try to keep in time to the music as they march.

The Three Billy-goats Gruff

> Counting to three, talking about sizes – and practising your phonic skills.

Resources

- Three goat masks
- Troll mask
- Bench for bridge
- A table draped with a cloth

Activity 1

Aims and objectives

- Tuning into voice sounds.
- Learning to distinguish between the differences in vocal sounds.

Preparation

- Read the story to the children using a higher or lower voice to differentiate between the different-sized billy-goats and a scary threatening voice for the troll as he asks,

  'Who's that walking over my bridge? I'm going to eat you up!'

- Arrange a bench to represent the bridge between the two fields.

What to do

- Choose three children to be the billy-goats and one to be the troll.
- The three billy-goats are together in one field with the troll sitting to the side of the bridge.
- As each billy-goat in turn crosses the bridge they are confronted by the troll.
- The largest billy-goat chases the troll away.
- The children can say the lines for their character in the character's voice as you read the story.

Activity 2

Aims and objectives

- Listening and remembering voice sounds.
- Learning to recognise and identify different voices.

Preparation

- Children should be seated in a large circle.

What to do

- Children take it in turns to come into the centre of the circle of children and speak the words.

  'I'm going over the bridge to eat the lovely green grass on the other side.'

- Choose one child to be the troll and sit under a table draped with a cloth.
- Can the troll tell from the voice whether the child is being the small, medium-sized or great big billy-goat?

Tip

These drama activities will adapt to fit many different fairy stories.

Songs

Adapt some old favourites to add some listening skills.

Resources

- Percussion instruments (all activities)

Activity 1

Aims and objectives

- Listening and remembering instrumental sounds.
- Learning to identify the differences between the sounds of different instruments.

Preparation

- Each child will need an instrument.
- Sit in a circle. If more than one child has a particular instrument they could sit together.

What to do

- To the tune of 'Peter hammers with one hammer' sing words that match the instruments you have.
- Ask the children to think about how they will play their instrument and choose a word that describes that action, e.g.

  We can beat the big drum, big drum, big drum,

  We can beat the big drum,

  Just like this.

  We can shake the shakers . . .

  We can tap the triangle . . .

  We can click the castanets . . .

- To the same tune make up some words to describe how you are playing. Encourage the children to find the best word to describe the different ways they can play, such as 'loudly', 'quietly', 'quickly', 'slowly', 'smoothly'. They could even create some new descriptive words, such as 'jumpily'.
- Sing and play your song:

  We can all play loudly, loudly, loudly,

  We can all play loudly,

  Just like this.

- Remind the children to match their playing to the words.

Tip

Every time you sing with the children you are offering them a chance to listen carefully, to notice the beat and the way that syllables in words correspond with the rhythm of the music, all part of the phonics curriculum as well as the children's creative development.

Activity 2

Aims and objectives

- Tuning into rhythm.
- Learning to understand the pattern of syllables.

Preparation

- Collect together some percussion instruments.
- Additional tuned instruments may be available, if not you will have to resort to pictures.

What to do

- Sing together.

  'I can play on the big bass drum, big bass drum, big bass drum,

  I can play on the big bass drum,

  In our nursery band.'

- Ask the children to suggest some other instruments that they might play in a nursery band.

- Accept all of their suggestions at first. Try to make them fit the rhythm – some may not work at all unless you say or sing the word in a funny way! Have a laugh with the children as you try to make them fit.

  'We can play the ke-ey board . . .'

  'We can play the be-e-ells . . .'

  'We can play the electric organ . . .'

- Explain to the children that you have to choose instruments that will keep the rhythm of this song correct. Remind them of 'big bass drum' Can they count the number of beats?
- This tells them that they have to choose instruments that have three beats in their name, e.g.

  cast-an-ets

  vi-o-lin

  xy-lo-phone

  tri-ang-le

  pi-an-o

  tam-bour-ine

  bass guit-ar.

- You may need to demonstrate some of the actions of playing these.
- Sing and mime different instruments as you sing.
- Now take your instruments and become a marching band. Sing and play as you march in a line behind the adult/conductor, all around the nursery grounds.

Activity 3

Aims and objectives

- Talking about instrumental sounds.
- Learning to develop a wide vocabulary to talk about musical sounds.

Preparation

- Sit in a circle.
- Each child has an instrument: a drum and drumstick, a shaker or a triangle and beater.

Tip

This is a chance to practise listening carefully and taking turns.

What to do

- This song adapts the words for 'If you're happy and you know it . . .'
- Children have to sing together, and play when it is their turn.
  If you're happy and you know it beat a drum . . .

  If you're happy and you know it and you really want to show it

  If you're happy and you know it beat a drum.

  If you're happy and you know it shake a shaker . . .

  If you're happy and you know it tap a triangle . . .

- In between these verses you can add something like:
  - 'If you're happy and you know it knock on wood' and the children can knock on the floor
  - 'If you're happy and you know it play a tune' and everyone plays at once.

Little Red Riding Hood

Take your drama outdoors for added realism.

Resources

- Red cloak and basket
- Wolf ears
- Grandma's nightie
- Toy axe

Activity 1

Aims and objectives

- Talking about voice sounds.
- Learning to talk about the different voices they can make and hear.

Preparation

- Read the story to the children using different voices for Red Riding Hood and the wolf.
- Encourage them to join in with the section of dialogue beginning – 'What big eyes you've got, Grandma.'
- Discuss how the wolf tries to disguise his voice to sound like Grandma.

What to do

- Choose a child to be Red Riding Hood and another to be the wolf and someone to be the woodcutter.
- Let Red Riding Hood pretend to walk through the woods with the wolf following her. The woodcutter can be watching from a distance. When Red Riding Hood stops to pick some flowers, the wolf hurries on to Grandma's cottage and holds the nightie in front of him.
- When Red Riding Hood arrives at the cottage they speak the dialogue exchange.
- The drama ends when the woodcutter chases the wolf away.

Activity 2

Aims and objectives

- Listening and remembering sounds they can make.
- Learning to create sounds for stories.

Preparation

- If you don't have trees or bushes within easy reach, the children could paint some trees and stick them to outside equipment. Or paint them directly onto the sides of large boxes to create a 'wood' outside.

What to do

- Talk with the children about what Red Riding Hood might hear or see as she walks through the wood. What other creatures live there and what noises do they make? E.g.
    mice
    squirrels
    bees
    birds
    deer
    rabbits.
- The children can work in pairs to choose a creature, work out how to make its sound and then hide somewhere in the wood you have created outside.
- One child can be dressed as Red Riding Hood, as she walks through the 'wood' she can hear lots of sounds. Can she identify the creatures?

Tip

Children should only make their noise when Red Riding Hood is passing their hiding place.

Appendices

Appendix 1

Treasure chest objects for the activities in **Pirates**, Part 2, Chapter 3

Sets of objects to use with the treasure chest, sorted by initial sound.
Each of these should be a real object or a toy replica.

/a/   apple, ant, alligator, axe

/ai/   acorn, alien, angel

/b/   bag, bib, boat, banana, ball, bed, bead, book, bird, bell

/k/   cup, cow, car, kitten, cord, kangaroo, comb, cone, king, Christmas tree, key, crayon, quoit

/d/   dog, doll, duck, dummy, disc, dish, dice, daffodil, dinosaur, dress

/e/   egg, elephant, engine, elf, elastic band, envelope

/ee/   Easter egg, eagle, ear, earring

/f/   farmer, photo, fan, feather, fish, fire, fork, fairy

/g/   goose, goat, gold, gate, garage, girl, glove, guitar, ghost

/h/   hat, house, horse, helicopter, heart, hedgehog, hook, handbag, helmet, handkerchief

/i/   igloo, insect, ink, invitation

/igh/   iron, ice cream, island, ivy

/j/   jug, jumper, giraffe, jewel, jam, jellyfish, jet, jigsaw

/l/   lamb, Lego®, ladder, lamp, leaf, lollipop, lemon, lime, lorry, lion, lipstick

/m/   mouse, mat, mug, magnet, mask, man, map, marble, motorbike, mirror, mitten

/n/   nappy, needle, nut, nurse, knitting, necklace, newt, newspaper

/o/   orange, ox, olive, oblong, octopus

/oa/   oval, ogre, oats

/p/ pig, pan, poppy, pencil, paper, pen, peg, paintbrush, pear, pine cone

/kw/ queen, quilt, quad bike

/r/ rat, ribbon, rabbit, raisin, rattle, roof, rhinoceros, ring, rocket

/s/ sock, soldier, sieve, cylinder, soap, sandal, spider, scarf, slide, spoon, square

/t/ towel, tissue, teapot, teddy, tiger, table, tambourine, telephone, television, toothbrush

/u/ umbrella, onion, underpants

/v/ van, vest, vase, violin

/w/ wizard, watch, window, wheel, whale, wand, wardrobe, washing machine, windmill

/y/ yellow, yacht, yam, yoghurt, yo-yo

/z/ zebra, zoo, zip, zero, zookeeper

/ch/ chocolate, chimney, chimpanzee, chain, chair, chick

/sh/ shoe, ship, shop, shark, shell, shed, shirt, shaker

/th/ three, thorn, thimble, thumb, thistle, throne

Appendix 2

Treasure chest objects for the activities in **Pirates**, Part 2, Chapter 3

Sets of objects that rhyme.
Each of these should be a real object or a toy replica – look in your small world toys (farm, doll's house, etc.) for many of these.

cat, rat, mat, hat, bat

dog, log, frog, hedgehog

car, bar, star, jar

pan, man, van, fan

tin, pin, bin, fin

chair, stair, pear, bear, square, hair

bag, rag, tag, Jag

boat, coat, goat, note, stoat

bed, red, Ted, shed

king, ring, wing, swing

dish, fish

egg, leg, peg, keg

fork, chalk, hawk

ink, drink, sink

jug, mug, rug, bug

lamb, ram, jam, ham

mouse, house

map, tap, cap, flap

ox, box, socks, chocs

queen, bean

zoo, shoe, two, kangaroo

shell, bell, well, hotel

bead, seed

bee, key, tree, three, monkey, donkey

hook, book

nurse, purse

spoon, moon, balloon

wheel, seal, heel, meal

toe, bow, dough, hoe

door, saw

blue, glue, shoe, loo

fly, pie, tie

skirt, shirt

tower, flower

brown, clown

doctor, tractor

face, lace, case

Appendix 3

Phonemes to graphemes (consonants)

Phoneme	Grapheme	Sample words
/b/	b bb	big, robber
/k/	c k ck	can, king, luck
/d/	d dd ed	doll, ladder, pushed
/f/	f ff ph	fin, huff, phone
/g/	g gg	get, digger
/h/	h	help
/j/	j g dg	jam, giant, hedge
/l/	l ll	long, tell
/m/	m mm	man, hammer
/n/	n nn	no, sunny
/p/	p pp	pull, nappy
/r/	r rr	red, parrot
/s/	s ss c	sing, hiss, circle
/t/	t tt ed	tub, hotter, bumped
/v/	v	voice
/w/	w	win
/y/	y	yell
/z/	z zz s se ze	zap, buzz, his, cheese, squeeze
/sh/	sh s ss t (before – ion/ial)	shed, sure, mission, station, martial
/ch/	ch tch	chin, pitch
/th/	th	thing
/th/	th	they
/ng/	ng n (before k)	bang, wink
/zh/	s (before – ion /ure)	vision, treasure

Phonemes to graphemes (vowels)

Phoneme	Grapheme	Sample words
/a/	a	and
/e/	e ea	elf, spread
/i/	i y	it, gym
/o/	o a	on, want
/u/	u o o-e	under, son, some
/ai/	ai ay a-e	train, pay, bake
/ee/	ee ea e ie	sweet, flea, she, thief
/igh/	igh ie y i-e i	light, tie, fly, like, find
/oa/	oa ow o oe o-e	coat, show, toe, go, phone
/oo/	oo ew ue u-e	hoop, new, blue, ruler
/oo/	oo u	book, shut
/ar/	ar a	arm, rather
/or/	or aw au ore al	for, claw, Paul, wore, walk
/ur/	ur er ir or (after w)	purse, her, bird, worm
/ow/	ow ou	now, shout
/oi/	oi oy	coin, toy
/air/	air are ear	hair, share, pear
/ear/	ear eer ere	near, beer, here
/ure/		sure, poor, tour
Inverted e		mother, doctor, cellar, treasure, metre

Adapted from tables 1 and 2 in *Letters and Sounds: Principles and Practice of High Quality Phonics*, DfES (2007).

Appendix 4

Aims and learning objectives

Based on *Letters and Sounds*, Phase One.

Aspects	Aim: Tuning into sounds	Aim: Listening & remembering sounds	Aim: Talking about sounds
1 **Environmental sounds**	To develop listening skills To be aware of sounds around them To recall sounds To discriminate between sounds To describe sounds	To develop vocabulary To identify sounds To imitate sounds	To place sounds in their context To identify sounds that are similar To talk about sounds
2 **Instrumental sounds**	To experience sounds made by musical instruments To develop awareness of the sounds made by different musical instruments To respond to musical sounds	To identify the differences between the sounds of different instruments To remember and repeat a rhythm To discriminate between loud and quiet sounds	To develop a wide vocabulary to talk about musical sounds To match sounds to instruments etc To use sound in imaginative ways To express an opinion about different sounds
3 **Body percussion (sounds we can make)**	To join in with words and actions in songs To keep in time make up patterns of sounds To recreate sounds with a variety of different rhythms, speed and volume	To distinguish between sounds To copy a pattern of sounds To remember patterns of sounds To identify sounds and their sources To create sounds for stories	To use a wide vocabulary to talk about sounds they can make To group sounds by a given criteria

Aspects	Aim: Tuning into sounds	Aim: Listening & remembering sounds	Aim: Talking about sounds
4 Rhythm and rhyme	To experience and enjoy rhythm and rhyme To be aware of rhythm and rhyme in speech To understand the pattern of syllables To repeat a rhyming string To recognise that some words rhyme	To be aware of words that rhyme To listen to and be aware of rhyming strings	To create their own rhymes To complete sentences using rhyming words To make up a series of rhyming words
5 Alliteration	To identify the initial sounds in words To reproduce initial sounds clearly To make up alliterative phrases	To hear the difference in sounds at the beginning of words To recall a list of objects that start with the same sound To suggest objects that start with the same sound To match sounds to objects	To know how different sounds are articulated To select a range of words that start with the same sound
6 Voice sounds	To distinguish between the differences in vocal sounds To articulate words carefully	To sustain listening To listen for a target word and respond with associated sound To remember a sound sequence To recognise and identify different voices	To widen the range of vocabulary needed to talk about the different voice and speech sounds they can make or hear
7 Oral blending & segmenting	To blend phonemes into words To say the word and identify the object it fits To blend words that start with the same initial phoneme	To listen to phonemes in words To remember the order of phonemes in words To segment words into phonemes	To talk about the different phonemes that make up a word To identify the number of phonemes in a given simple word

References

Official documents

DfES (2007) *Practice Guidance for the Early Years Foundation Stage. Non-statutory Guidance*. Ref: 00012-2007

DfES (2007) *Letters and Sounds: Principles and Practice of High Quality Phonics*. Ref: 00282-2007

Rose, J. (2006) *Independent Review of the Teaching of Early Reading. Final report*. Ref: 0201-2006

www.standards.dfes.gov.uk/rosereview

Picture books

Andreae, G. and Sharratt, N. (2003) *Pants*, London: Picture Corgi

Andreae, G. and Wojtowycz, D. (1998) *Rumble in the Jungle*, London: Orchard Books

Browne, E. (1995) *Handa's Surprise*, London: Walker Books

Burningham, J. (1992) *Come Away from the Water, Shirley*, Red Fox, London: Random House Children's Books

Burningham, J. (1979) *Mr Gumpy's Motor Car*, London: Picture Puffins

Burningham, J. (1978) *Mr Gumpy's Outing*, London: Picture Puffins

Bush, J. and Korky, P. (1991) *The Fish Who Could Wish*, Oxford: Oxford University Press

Butterworth, N. and Inkpen, M. (1993) *Jasper's Beanstalk*, London: Hodder Children's Books

Campbell, R. (1984) *Dear Zoo*, Picture Puffins, London: Penguin

Hughes, S. (2002) *Alfie Weather*, Red Fox Books, London: Random House Children's Books

Hutchins, P. (1975) *Good-night, Owl!*, London: Picture Puffins

Hutchins, P. (2001) *Rosie's Walk*, Red Fox Books, London: Random House Children's Books

Kubler, A. (2007) *The Wheels on the Bus go Round and Round*, Swindon: Child's Play International

Martin, B. and Carle, E. (1994) *Polar Bear, Polar Bear, What Do You Hear?* London: Picture Puffins

Mayo, M and Aycliffe, A. (2005) *Choo, Choo, Clickety Clack*, London: Orchard Books

Melling, D (2008) *Two by Two and a Half*, London: Hodder Children's Books

Murphy, J. (1995) *Peace at Last*, London: Macmillan Children's Books

Murphy, J. (1995) *Whatever Next!*, London: Macmillan Children's Books

Pelham, D. (1993) *Sam's Sandwich*, London: Random House (UK)

Prater, J. (1984) *On Friday Something Funny Happened*, London: Puffin

Rosen, M. and Reynolds, A. (2007) *The Bear in the Cave*, London: Bloomsbury Publishing Plc

Rosen, M. and Oxenbury, H. (1995) *We're Going on a Bear Hunt*, London: Walker Books

Ross, T. (1995) *Stone Soup*, London: Picture Lions (an imprint of HarperCollins Publishers Ltd)

Sharratt, N. (2006) *Don't Put your Finger in the Jelly, Nelly*, London: Scholastic Ltd

Showers, P. and Aliki (illustrator) (1991) *The Listening Walk*, HarperCollins (in the series HarperTrophy)

Simmons, J. (2005) *Daisy and the Moon*, London: Orchard Books

Sutton, E. (1978) *My Cat Likes to Hide in Boxes*, London: Puffin

Sykes, J. and Warnes, T. (1996) *I Don't Want to go to Bed*, London: Little Tiger Press (an imprint of Magi publications)

Your own choice of fairy story books

Poems and rhymes

Bennett, J (compiler) (1989) *Singing in the Sun*, London: Puffin
        'Sailing to sea' by Dennis Lee

Evans, D. (1988) *Fingers, Feet and Fun*, London: Beaver Book, Arrow Books Ltd (an imprint of Century Hutchinson Ltd)
        '5 big crackers in a box'

Foster, J. (chosen by) (1995) *Blue Poetry Paintbox*, Oxford: Oxford University Press

'I wish I was a pirate' by Tony Bradman

'There was an old pirate' by Wendy Larmont

Gliori, D. (illustrator) (1999) *Noisy Poems*, London: Walker Books

'Early in the morning' Anon

'Laughing time' by William Jay Smith

'City Music' by Tony Mitton

Rosen, M. (1985) *Don't*, London: Andre Deutsch Ltd

Rumble, A. (compiler) (1989) *Is a Caterpillar Ticklish?* London: Puffin

'Bubble' by Jacqueline Segal

'Jump or jiggle' by Evelyn Beyer

'Shadow dance' by Ivy O. Eastwick

'Soap bubbles' by Maisie Cobb

Matterson, E (compiler) (1991) *This Little Puffin*, London: Penguin

Counting rhymes etc.

Your own choice of nursery rhyme books

Music

'Slowly, slowly walks my grandad' in (1983) *Tinder-box. 66 Songs for Children*, London: A&C Black

Extracts from these or any similar pieces of music:

'Mars' from *The Planets* by Holst

'The Dance of the Sugar Plum Fairy' from *The Nutcracker* ballet by Tchaikovsky

The Washington Post by John Philip Sousa

'Nellie the elephant' comic song

'The Sting' by Scott Joplin

'The Typewriter' by Leroy Anderson

'The Blue Danube' by Johann Strauss

'The Swan' from *Carnival of the Animals* by Saint-Saëns

'The Tritsch Tratsch Polka' by Johann Strauss

'Entrance of the Gladiators' by Julius Fucik

Art

Goldfish by Henri Matisse

The Monkeys (or *Surprised*) by Henri Rousseau

The Great Wave by Katsushika Hokusu

The Cholmondeley Sisters (artist unknown)

The Visitor by Arthur Hopkins

Copies of these pictures are easily available via the internet.